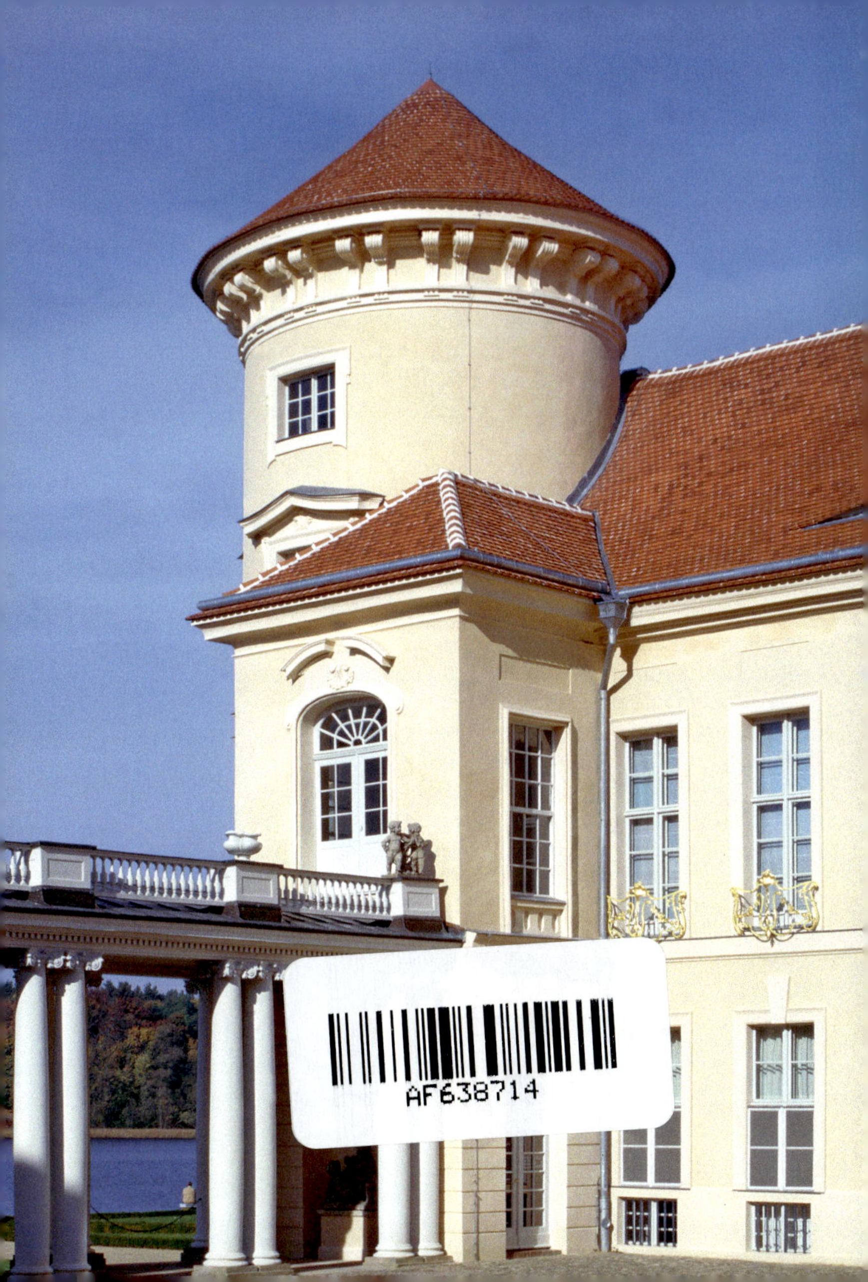

On the site of the present-day palace there was already a moated castle in the 13th century, which served as a border fortress for the protection of the northern part of the Marches of Brandenburg against Mecklenburg. After the estate had changed hands several times a house in the Renaissance style was built here, which King Friedrich Wilhelm I (1688–1740) bought as a residence for his eldest son, Crown Prince Friedrich (1712–1786) in March 1734.

After the disputes between the King and his son, which lasted for many years and which culminated in the Crown Prince's unsuccessful attempt to escape and his subsequent imprisonment at the fortress in Küstrin had been settled, and Friedrich had consented to marry Princess Elisabeth Christine von Braunschweig-Bevern, the Crown Prince was appointed commander of the infantry regiment von der Goltz in Neuruppin in 1732.

It can be assumed that Friedrich with the knowledge of the area acquired while stationed as an officer in Neuruppin influenced the choice of Rheinsberg as his future residence. After Friedrich Wilhelm had bought the estate for his son, he commissioned the Brandenburg Director of Building Works Johann Gottfried Kemmeter, to convert the house. The overall design provided for the enlargement of the Renaissance building to form a house with three wings ending in round towers and linked by a colonnade on the side facing the lake. The extension of the building began with the Klingenberg wing – whose name goes back to a striking clock previously mounted here. This wing housed the apartments of the Crown Prince. The newly erected corps de logis replaced the old gatehouse.

In August 1736 work on the Klingenberg wing was so far advanced that the Crown Prince and his consort were able to move from Ruppin to Rheinsberg. The building works as a whole, however, continued

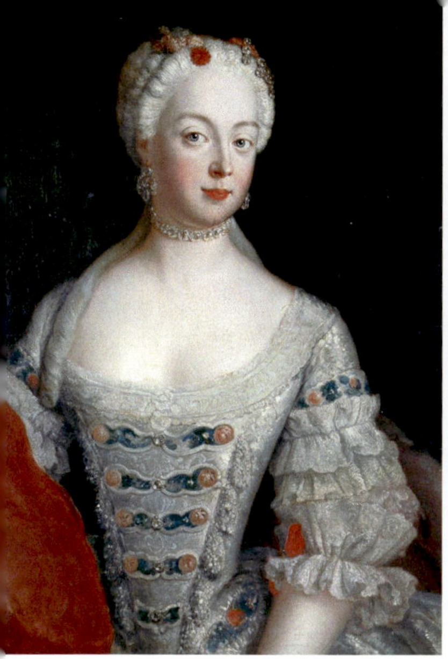

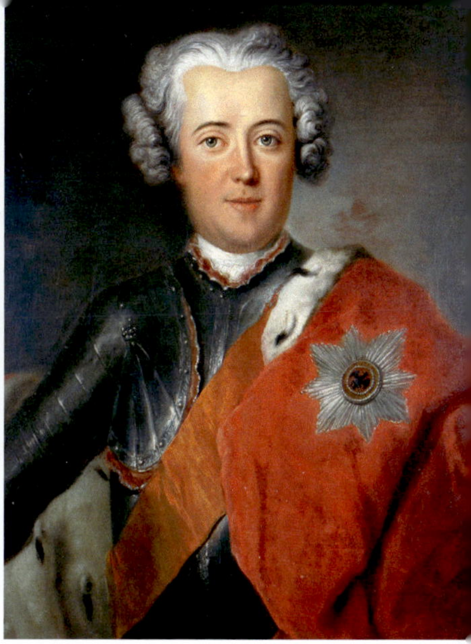

Antoine Pesne: *Crown Princess Elisabeth Christine,* 1738

Antoine Pesne: *Crown Prince Friedrich,* 1738

until 1740. The completion of the house by the construction of the north wing with the second tower was taken over from 1737 by Georg Wenzeslaus von Knobelsdorff, after he had completed a study tour of Italy with the support of the Crown Prince. At this stage, however, he was no longer able to influence the overall design of the palace. His improvements in the design of the façades and above all his designs for the decoration of the interiors were, however, of considerable importance. In conjunction with the laying out of the palace gardens from 1734, which like all the later Friderician gardens were both decorative and utilitarian, the development of Friderician Rococo began in Rheinsberg, which only a few years later reached its artistic apogee in Charlottenburg and above all Sanssouci

The Rheinsberg years of Crown Prince Friedrich were often described as idyllic in later historical and literary descriptions. He himself lent credence to this

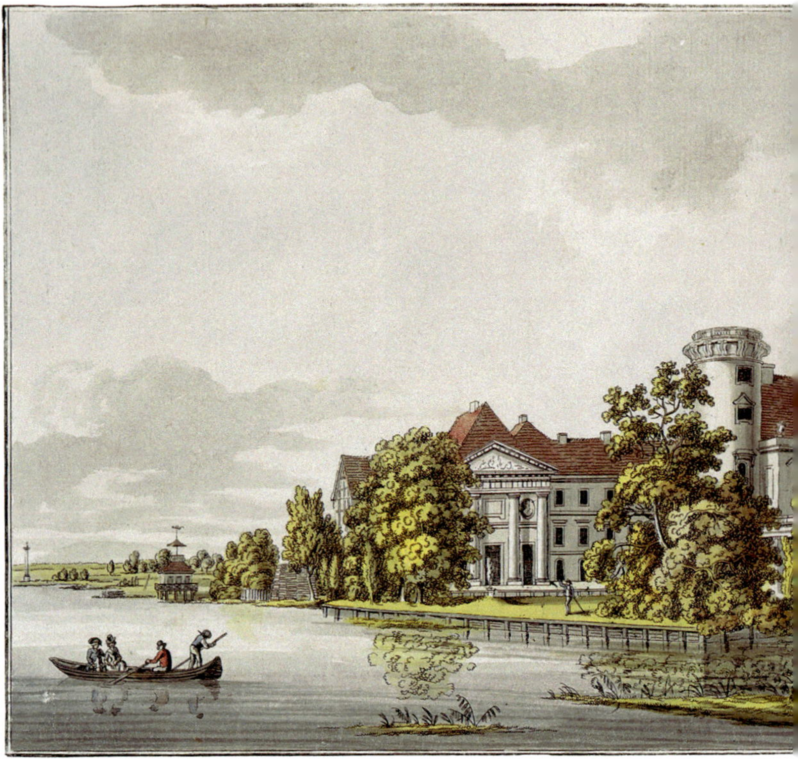

Benjamin Schwarz: Palace with Theatre Wing, c. 1790

view by enthusiastic remarks in poems and letters from »Remusberg«. Shortly before his death the King confessed that he had spent the happiest years of his life in Rheinsberg. In these years he led a relatively independent and free life which gave him the opportunity to follow his personal inclinations and his own ideas.

Music played an important part at the court in Rheinsberg. The Crown Prince's orchestra brought together excellent soloists and composers such as the brothers Graun and Benda. For a time Friedrich's flute

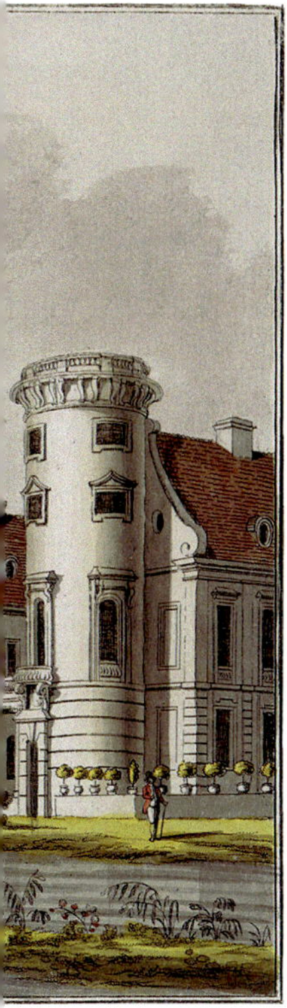



teacher, Johann Joachim Quantz was a guest at court. Only a few select cultivated and trusted people were among the Crown Prince's closest friends in Rheinsberg – his secretary, the French cleric Jordan, Baron de la Motte-Fouqué, his amusing companion, Freiherr von Keyserlingk, von Suhm, the former Saxon envoy to Berlin, and the architect Baron von Knobelsdorff. Apart from the numerous amusements, it was above all the intensive study of history, philosophy, religion and politics that occupied the Crown Prince in these years. He was particularly interested in classical poets and philosophers – Lucretius, Horace, Virgil, Seneca, Marcus Aurelius, for example. Two days after the move to Rheinsberg he began to exchange letters with Voltaire, the disputatious French writer and philosopher, whom the Crown Prince passionately admired. His interest in politics is reflected mainly in *Antimachiavell* written in Rheinsberg in 1739 in which Friedrich dealt critically with Machiavelli's treatise *Il Principe* (The Prince, 1552). He set his own idea of the ruler as »the first servant of the state« against the thesis of the Italian that all means are permitted to the state in the preservation of its power.

Having succeeded to the throne after the death of his father in 1740, Friedrich took the decision to extend Potsdam as his summer residence and gave the Rheinsberg estate to his brother Heinrich (1726–1802) in 1744. Heinrich, who was very similar to the King in character and also in his military, philosophical and artistic inclinations, found it difficult »as a prince of the royal blood« to accustom himself to his subordinate role in the hierarchy of the royal family. Initially, it was the condescension of Friedrich II which he felt to be unbearable, who from 1740 stepped into his father's shoes and took on the education and upbringing of his much younger brother. Later there were vehement arguments above all on military questions which put a strain on the relationship between the King and Prince during the wars of those years. However, Friedrich the Great greatly valued his brother's unusual diplomatic and military skill. Hardly any other Prussian prince was received with such honours and had such honours bestowed on him on his visits to European royal courts. It was only Friedrich's objection which deprived Prince Heinrich of the Polish royal crown, which was twice offered to him. He himself turned down a regency or governorship in the United States of America, which was likewise offered to him. Without his own court for which a Prussian prince was eligible only after marriage, Heinrich could at first not live permanently at Rheinsberg. But in July 1746 he received his royal brother, his mother Sophie Dorothea and his sister Princess Amalie for a brief visit to Rheinsberg as the new master of the house. For Friedrich, this was the last visit to his former residence as Crown Prince.

It was only the marriage – favoured by Friedrich – of Heinrich to Princess Wilhelmine von Hessen-Kassel in 1752 which afforded the Prince relative autonomy and permitted him to reside in Rheinsberg. In the subsequent five decades Rheinsberg was where Heinrich preferred to be. For a long time his presence in Rheinsberg was only interrupted by his involvement in military conflict and his extensive journeys to Sweden, Russia and France.

The Prince shared his royal brother's love of French culture and way of life, and also his love of architecture, landscape gardening, literature, music and theatre. A new palace theatre with a remarkable early neo-classical interior was installed in 1774 under the supervision of the Director of Building Works, Carl Wilhelm Hennert in the west side-wing, which was originally erected by von Knobelsdorff as servants' quarters and which was later used as accommodation for the royal household. The opera and theatre performances which took place two to three

Corps de Logis, with sculptures by Friedrich Christian Glume on the attica

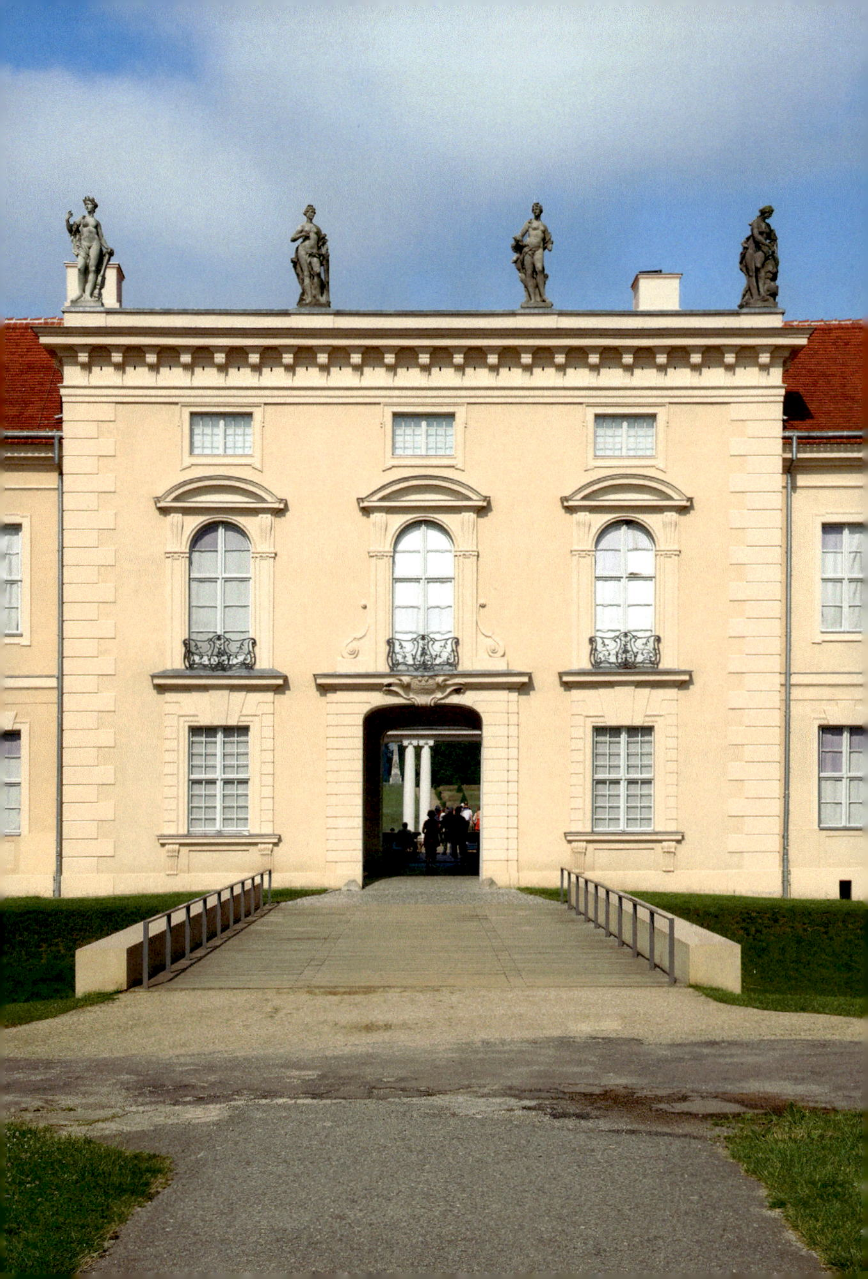

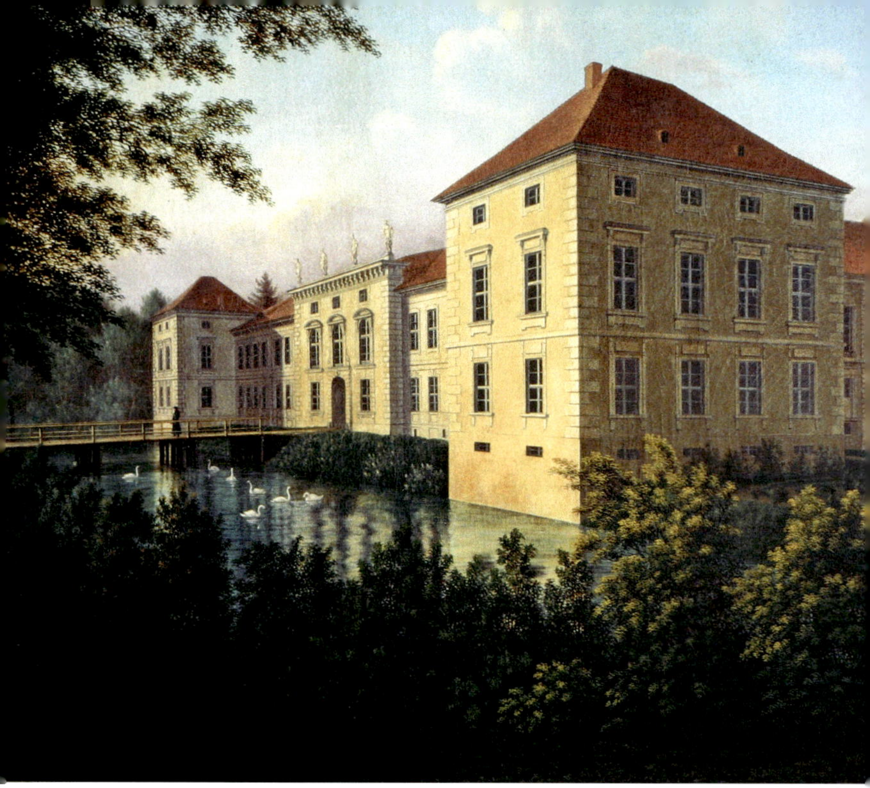

Wilhelm Barth, Schloss Rheinsberg, c. 1842/42

times a week even attracted audiences to Rheinsberg from Berlin.

After 1789 Prince Heinrich granted asylum at his court to numerous French émigrés who were fleeing from political events in their country. Externally the palace building largely retained the form as completed by von Knobelsdorff. Only the addition of two corner pavilions in 1785/86 impaired the overall balanced effect of the architecture. After Prince Heinrich's death in 1802 the two towers were given their present conical roofs.

The changes to the interiors were, however, all the more radical and the ground plan and interior

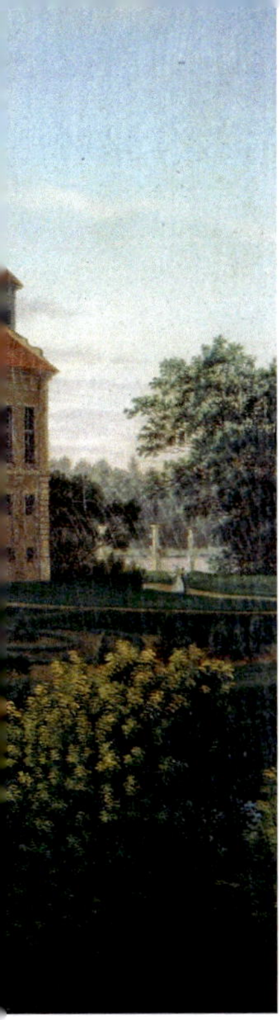

decoration were in part completely redesigned. The décors from the time of Crown Prince Friedrich were preserved in only five rooms. The changes and extensions commissioned by Prince Heinrich especially after 1763 still characterise the appearance of the palace and park. While the young architect Carl Gotthard Langhans from Wroclaw was staying at Rheinsberg in 1766 he produced a number of drawings for remodelling the apartment of Princess Wilhelmine – which was later called Ferdinand's apartment after one of Heinrich's brothers – and for redesigning the staircase and the Shell Room in which elements of the transitional style from Rococo to neo-classicism already predominate. In the following years work was above all devoted to creating a summer apartment for the Prince on the ground floor of the Klingenberg wing and in the corps de logis. Rheinsberg saw a final high point in interior design after 1786 in the early neo-classical décor of the Prince's bedchamber, the Long Chamber and the library. Apart from the expansion and ornamentation of the park, the creation of a great system of avenues opening up the surrounding landscape, the continued design and construction of the town – above all its three public squares – were an integral part of the comprehensive design concept for Prince Heinrich's residence.

Prince Heinrich died on 3 August 1802 and was buried in the pyramid tomb. Rheinsberg was given to his brother Ferdinand. The large art collection of the deceased was sold in large part at several public auctions. After Ferdinand's death his son Prince August inherited the house and estate in 1813, in which his wife Auguste von Prillwitz lived for part of the time. On the the death of August the Rheinsberg estate went to the Prussian royal family as crown property (Fideikommisbesitz) in 1843 and was placed under the administration of the Hofkammer (office of financial administration) until 1945. From the middle of the 19th century writers and artists like Theodor Fontane, Adolph Menzel, Andrew Hamilton and Kurt Tucholsky increasingly drew the attention of early tourism to this place. From 1945 the palace was no longer accessible as a museum. After various interim uses to which it was put a sanatorium was installed in the palace and outbuildings in 1950. On 1 April 1991 the Stiftung Staatliche Schlösser und Gärten Potsdam-Sanssouci (Foundation of state-owned palaces and gardens at Potsdam-Sanssouci), a precursor of the present-day Stiftung Preußische Schlösser und Gärten Berlin-Brandenberg, took over the estate and only a few weeks later on 6 May opened the palace museum. In 1993 the Foundation also took over the gardens. It was also possible to open the Galerie für zeitgenössische Kunst (Gallery of contemporary art) and one year later the Kurt Tucholsky Memorial Centre (now the literary museum) to visitors in the basement of the north wing of the palace (the former apartment of the steward).

The extensive works begun in 1991 to restore the fabric of the palace and the restoration of the interiors will be continued steadily in the years to come.

Friedrich had the Renaissance palace at Rheinsberg extended to form a building with three wings, which on the side facing away from the town opens via the *cour d'honneur* to Lake Grienerick and the landscape beyond, much in the manner of Sanssouci at a later date. The main avenue begins – just as in Sanssouci – with an ornamental garden gate, flanked by Flora and Pomona, and leads via a sunken orangerie parterre to the central projection of the south side wing. On either side of this avenue hedged enclosures were created for fruit trees and mazes. From here the long transverse avenue leads over a former canal to a garden room formerly conceived as an orangerie. In the north towards the lake Heinrich had bosquet rooms with straight paths laid out, leading to piazza-like cabinets. To the south kitchen gardens were created.

The early Friderician work in Rheinsberg shows distinct features of the Rococo, a striving for intimacy and startling changes of impression. Pleasure gardens and kitchen gardens were combined. The gar-

Heckentheater (theatre in hedge enclosures) in Rheinsberg Garden

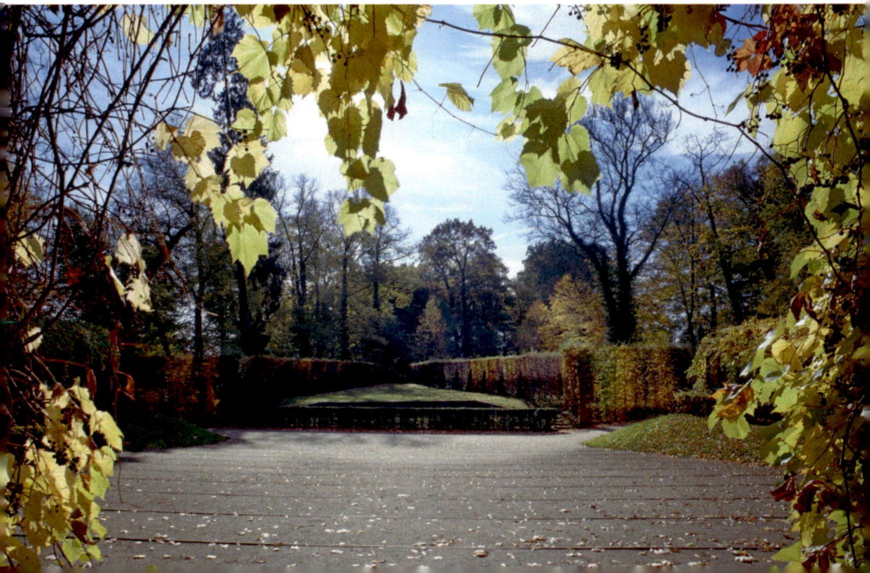

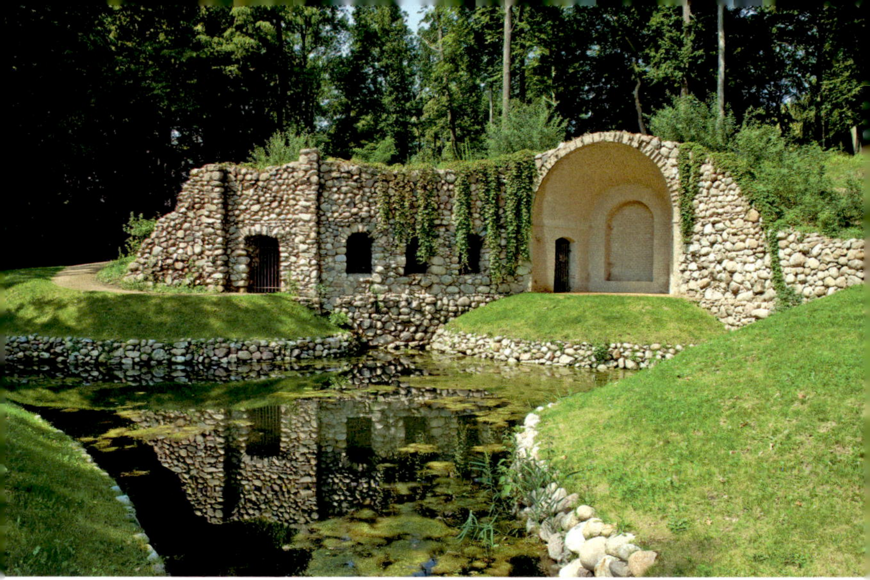

Egeria Grotto

dens are arranged in small rooms along the banks, open up on several sides of the palace and lead an independent life of their own. The landscape was integrated like a picture into the gardens. In Rheinsberg Friedrich sought the world of the »fêtes galantes« and country life, which appealed to him »a thousand times more than life in the town and at court«.

In 1752 Heinrich began to extend the gardens to the west, and – parallel to the grottos in Sanssouci – and in 1753 he had the rock grotto, a Chinese house and a theatre in the hedge enclosures constructed. He also created a star-shaped system of avenues in parts of the Boberow Woods that he had bought, and erected a treillis-work cabinet there. Many of these architectural features were lost after his death in 1802. A woodland path through the so-called Boberow-Kabeln and Boberow Park still reminds the visitor of former staffages and follies like the tomb of Virgil, the Temple of Friendship, the Dairy, the Rousseau monument or the sprucewood lodge. Heinrich's let-

Pyramid tomb of Prince Heinrich

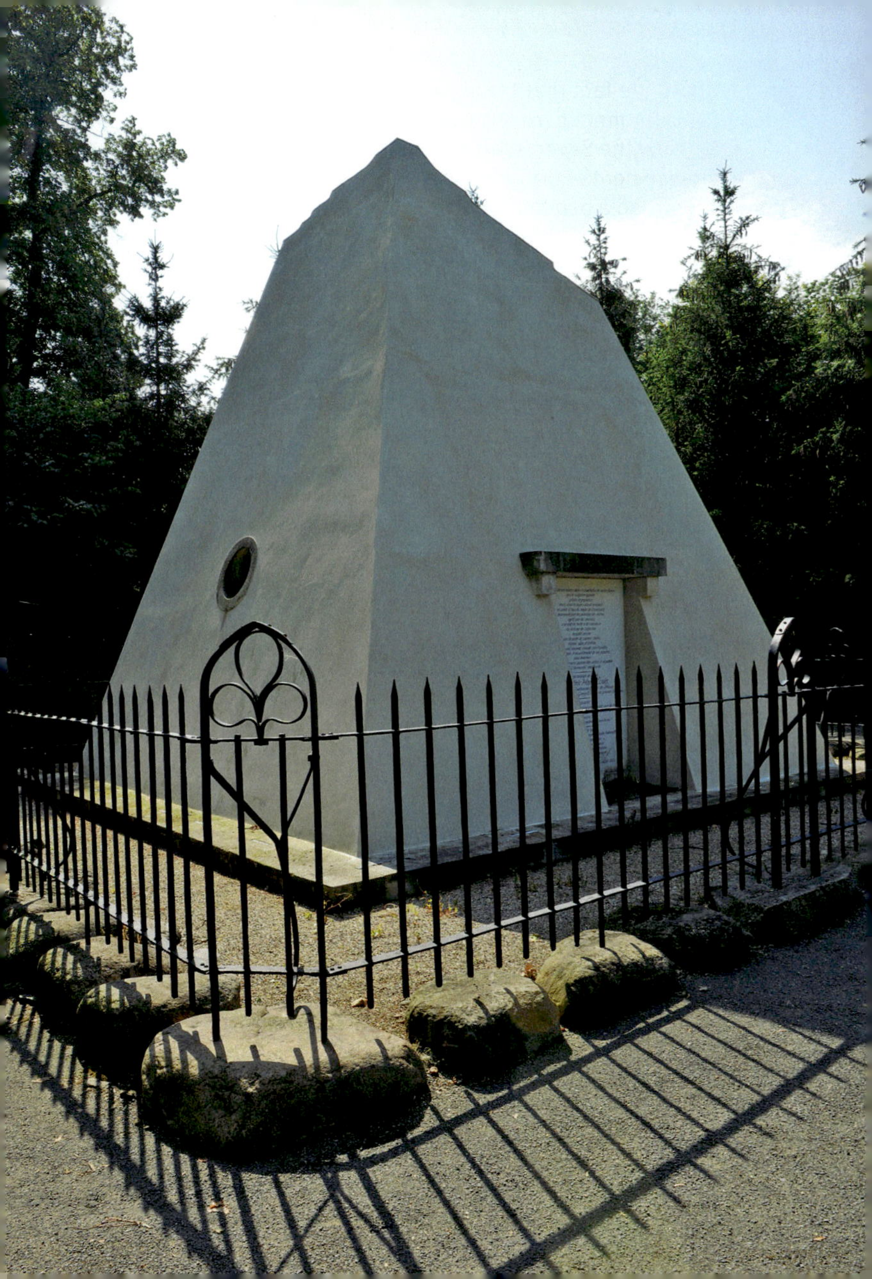

ters testify to the fact that there was dancing and a mood of enchantment here until deep into the night.

In 1763, after the Seven Years War, further projects for the improvement of the Rheinsberg park followed. Thus Heinrich had a painted Trajan column erected as an eyecatcher opposite the palace on the meanwhile raised terraces on the shore of the lake in honour of the heroes of the war where in 1791 an obelisk was erected. Further to the north kitchen gardens as the expression of a playfully decorative horticulture were linked by curving or serpentine paths. Likewise there was a dairy on the shore with a painted Concordia Temple whose ruins still remind the visitor of its former existence. In 1764 Prince Heinrich ordered marble columns in Italy to decorate the island in the lake with large flower baskets. After the French Revolution the Temple of Friendship, memorials with sentimental inscriptions, the Egeria Grotto as the focal point at the end of the large transverse avenue and finally his own tomb in the form of a pyramid were erected.

Heinrich's designs proclaimed new ideals. Thus the paths still lead irregularly and without system through the park according to Hogarth's »serpentine lines of beauty«. Nevertheless, Rococo features still predominate as adaptations of the formal repertoire of the Baroque. The design concept is revealed in the freely growing crowns of trees behind regular hedges, or in the use of green groves, corridors, arbours, marquees and huts. The Rheinsberg gardens represent an important, early and mature example of the Rococo in Germany, in which it is still possible to sense the relationship of that period to nature in its predilection for the representation of the gods and muses of Antiquity on the one hand, the love of pastorals, secret festivities and playful light-heartedness on the other. The small gardens are still rooms in which to experience the exotic, lightness and delicate elegance.

The visitor reception area with the museum shop are located in the former stables opposite the palace and on the ground floor of the corps de logis to the north of the entrance **driveway** (**Rooms 64, 65**). These rooms originally belonged to the apartments of ladies in waiting.

In the main season the north side **staircase** (**Room 5**) serves as the visitor staircase to the rooms of the palace. This area of the upper storey decorated in scagliola gave access from the apartments of the Crown Prince in the Klingenberg wing situated opposite to the Great Hall via the colonnade.

## UPPER STOREY

The Great Hall also known as the **Hall of Mirrors** (**Room 3**) with the antechamber and the Bacchus Cabinet, which have been largely preserved in their original décor, are among the earliest examples of Friderician interior decoration. They were completed under the direction of Georg Wenzeslaus von Knobelsdorff (1739/1740).

The hall, which extends the entire width of the wing, is given a light and airy impression by the arrangement of windows on the long sides and the west end wall. The complex refraction of light on the surface of Lake Grienerick is enhanced by the window pillars fitted with mirrors and the two trumeau mirrors of the mantlepieces, whose gilded frames have not been preserved. The walls clad in light scagliola, structured by Corinthian pilasters on the end walls and gilded ornamentation enhance this atmospheric effect. The vaulted ceiling in pink with gilded stucco ornamentation frames the ceiling which opens up in the form of the celestial firmament. In the corners it is decorated with musical emblems while the white cherub reliefs in the central reserves represent alle-

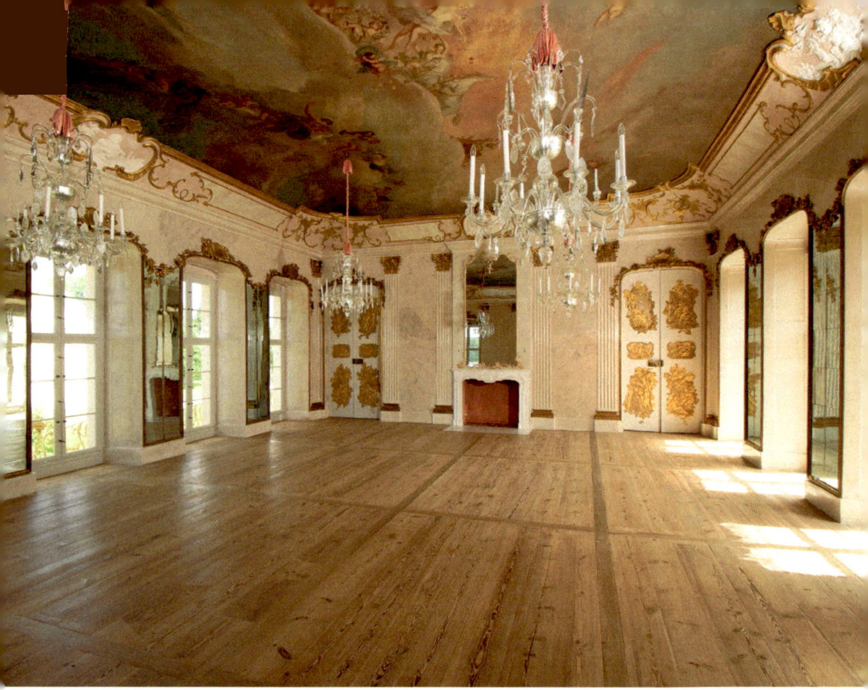

Hall of Mirrors

gories of the four seasons. The ceiling painting *Der Tag vertreibt die Finsternis (the day dispels the dark)* signed in 1740 by the artist Antoine Pesne with floral paintings by Augustin Dubuisson was repeatedly interpreted as an allegory of the imminent accession of Friedrich (II). The doors with gilded reliefs (presumably executed by Johann Carl Scheffler) show scenes from Ovid's Metamorphoses and are a direct pointer to the intended use of the room as a concert hall: music transforms man.

**The Tower or Bacchus Cabinet** (**Room 4**) retained the original décor of 1739/40 with the ceiling painting *Ganymed wird von Hebe im Olymp empfangen (Ganymed received by Hebe on Mount Olympus)* by Antoine Pesne, with the walls in white scagliola adorned with carved and gilded ornament with vine

Antechamber

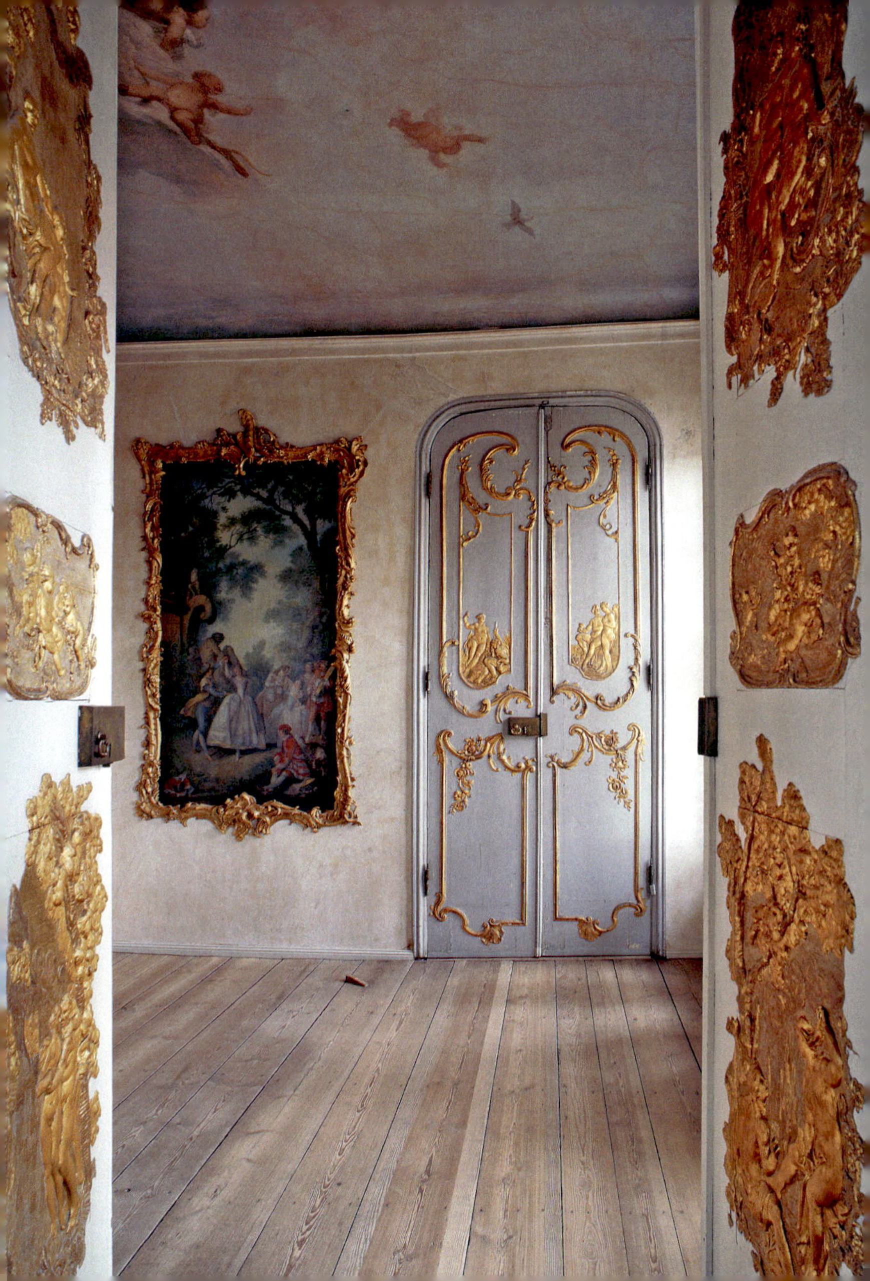

leaves and divine attributes above the door and window embrasures and with the floorboards typical of Rheinsberg at the time of the Crown Prince. The mantelpiece in grey marble was removed after 1945 but after 2002 fragments were reinstalled. Instead of the missing trumeau mirror there is a portrait of Crown Prince Friedrich by Georg Wenzeslaus von Knobelsdorff (c. 1735).

**The Antechamber** (**Room 2**) with its likewise preserved Friderician décor (1739/40) was the entrance to the Great Hall. The design aimed to evoke a suitable atmosphere to entice the courtly party into the adjacent Banqueting Hall. Thus, in the ceiling painting Antoine Pesne introduces »the gods of love which desire to harness doves to the chariot of Venus«. The two integrated wall paintings with gilded carved frames *Konzert im Freien (concert in the open air)* and *Tanz im Freien (dance in the open air)* (by an unknown artist in the manner of Watteau) underline the intended effect. On the doors there are scenes from Ovid's Metamorphoses.

## Apartment of Princess Amalie (Rooms 6 to 8)

In 1756 Prince Heinrich had the rooms originally used by the ladies in waiting to the Crown Princess converted and re-decorated for the planned visit of his sister Princess Amalie in 1762.

The wall covering of the **Red Chamber** (**Room 6**) was renewed in 1985 in the Friderician lace ribbon pattern. The gilded stucco rosette was complemented at the end of the $18^{th}$ century by a laurel wreath which points to the intended function of the room as a memorial to Prussian and French military commanders whom Heinrich venerated. The gallery, which originally consisted of eight portraits of military com-

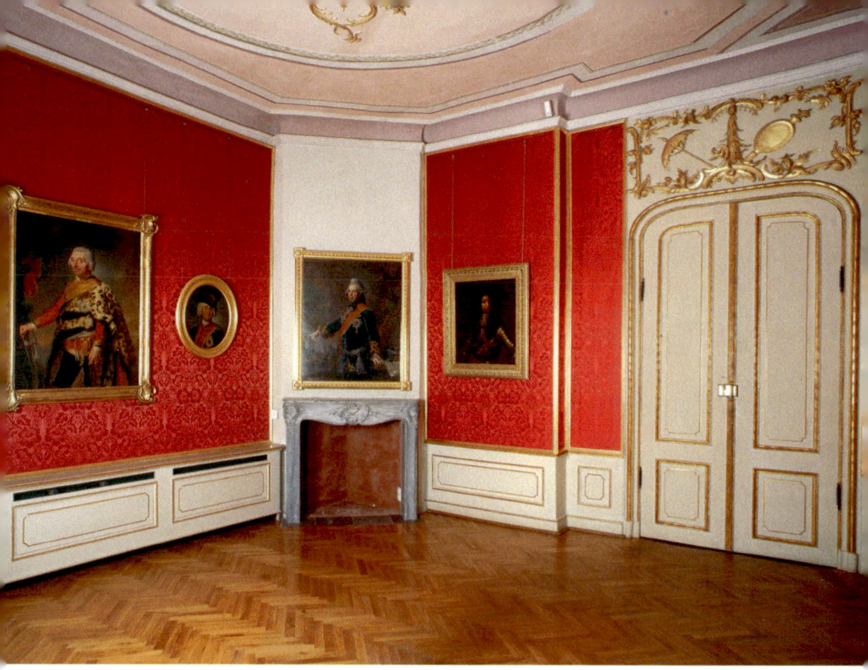

Amalie's apartment, Red Chamber with portrait gallery of military commanders

manders, is today complemented by a painting by Johann Heinrich Tischbein the Elder (1769), which portrays Prince Heinrich as the victor of the Battle of Freiberg.

The four sections of an East Asian screen in red lacquer technique, which were set in the boiserie behind glass and which have been preserved in their original position, are the main ornament of the **Lacquer Cabinet** (**Room 7**), which is completely decorated in the Chinoiserie style. The ceiling with a gilded stucco rosette, the supraportes and doors with gilded carvings, the two trumeau mirrors and the marquetry flooring were part of the original fittings of the room. Originally, there were 30 wall consoles in the cabinet displaying East Asian porcelain.

At the end of this suite of rooms there is the **Bedchamber** (**Room 8**) with the alcove where the bed with

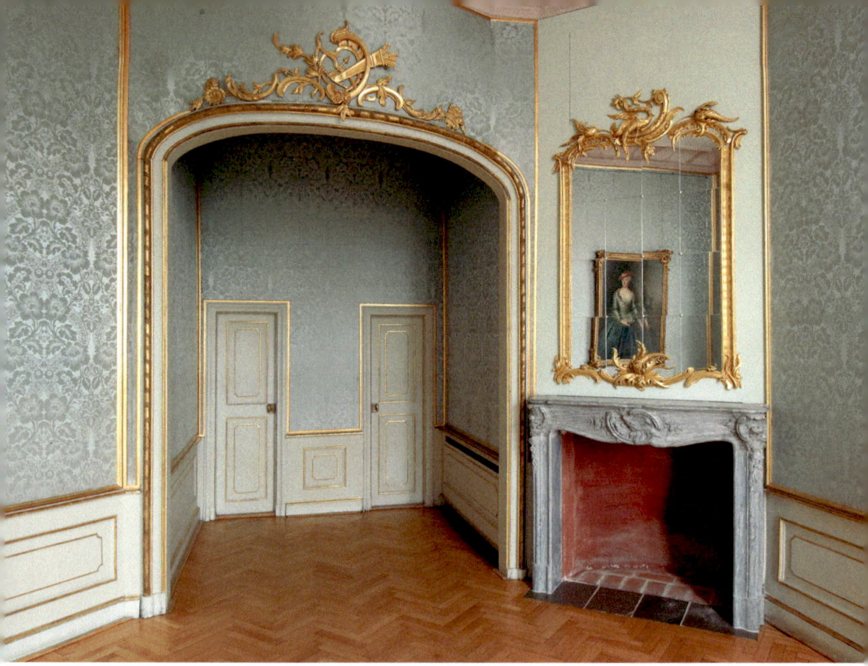

Amalie's apartment, bedchamber

hangings mentioned in the inventory of 1802 stood. The painting listed in the inventory of 1802 as »Kniestück, *die Königin von Schweden Ulrica Louise«* (sister of Friedrich II) has since 1991 again hung in the bedchamber which was painstakingly restored from 1985 onwards (Antoine Pesne, *Prinzessin Luise Ulrike von Schweden als Schäferin, Princess Luise Ulrike of Sweden as a Shepherdess)* (1738).

## North Pavilion/Apartment of the Marquise de Sabran (Rooms 10 to 15)

During his visits to Paris Prince Heinrich met the Marquise de Sabran. From 1791–1797 she lived as an émigrée at the Rheinsberg court and had her apartment on the piano nobile of the pavilion facing the

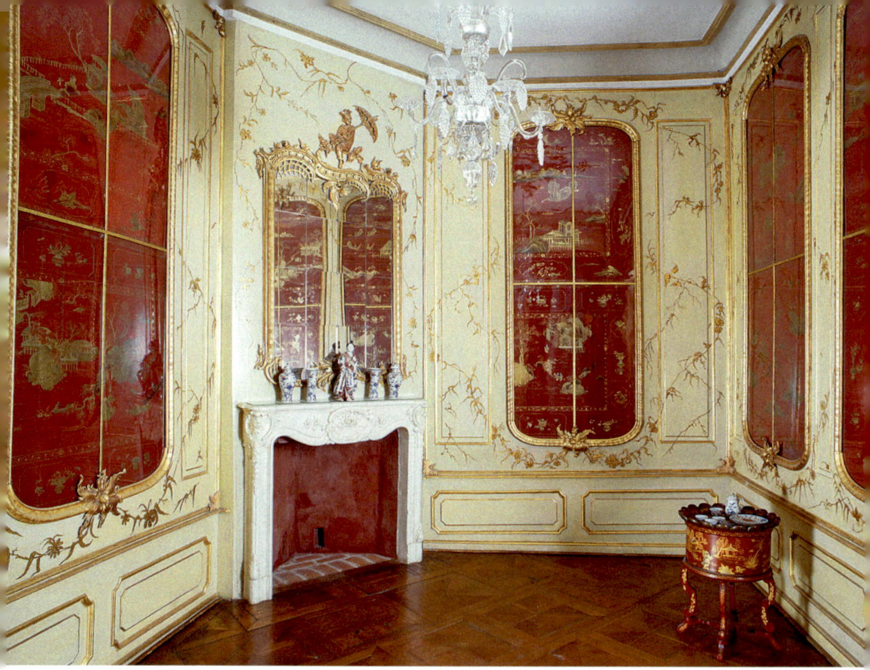

Amalia's apartment, lacquer cabinet

town. However, the building in its present condition is part of a new building by Karl Friedrich Schinkel which became necessary in 1825/26 as the pavilion, which had been added as recently as 1786, had been built on inadequate foundations. Essentially, the rooms still exhibit the decoration executed in the 19th century. Fragments of the historic wallpapers are preserved behind the neutral paint on the walls. The rooms are used for the presentation of the history of the palace and have no historic fittings.

## Apartment of Prince Ferdinand (Rooms 20 to 25)

In place of the rooms furnished as apartments for ladies in waiting until 1740, an apartment was created in 1767, presumably according to designs by Carl Gotthard Langhans, for the consort of Prince Heinrich, which, however, was later used only by Prince Ferdinand.

In the former **Room for ladies in waiting** (**Rooms 20/21**) fragments of the wall decoration before 1740 have been discovered and preserved. The ceiling with mouldings, cornice and vault, the painted panelling, marbelising on the walls, windows and flooring have been preserved from the building period under Crown Prince Friedrich. In keeping with the original décor with family portraits, today a series of portraits of the brothers and sisters of Friedrich II by Thomas Huber (1740) are displayed.

In the **Bedchamber** (**Room 22**) the wall panelling with a painted rhomboid pattern on a silver ground, the silver-painted stucco of the ceiling and the marble mantlepiece from the period after 1767 have been preserved. In the course of extensive restoration (completed 2005) a complete impression of the room was recreated.

A bergère next to the bed »with baldachin« was mentioned in the inventory of 1802. The fauteuil, which is now part of the furnishings, came from Berlin/Potsdam (around 1765). With the exception of the two supraportes with floral still-lifes by Augustin Dubuisson the rest of the fixed décor of the **Cabinet** (**Room 23**) with painted floral garlands on the wall panelling and the ceiling with stucco ornamentation has been retained. Of the nine wall consoles on which soapstone figures were displayed, four have been preserved.

**The Audience Room** (**Room 24**) was created in 1767 by joining together two previous rooms for ladies in waiting. The ceiling is ornamented with gilded and painted stucco which was designed to match the dark-blue damask covered walls (reconstruction 2002).

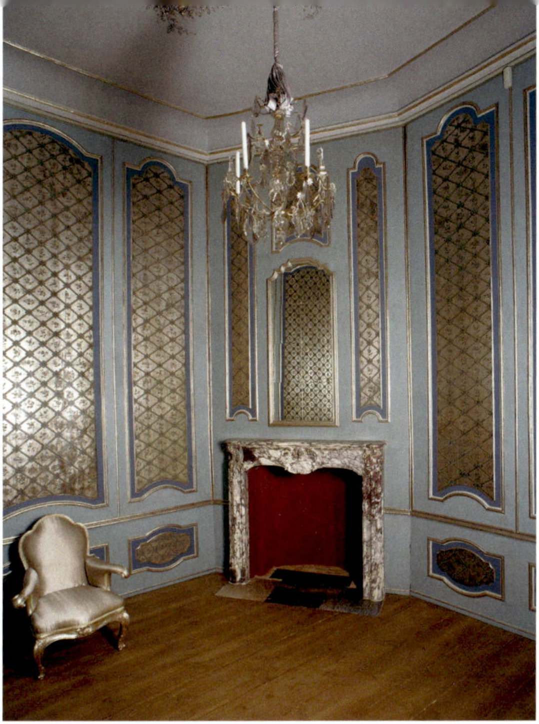

Ferdinand's apartment, bedchamber

In 1776, on his second visit to Russia, Prince Heinrich received five St. Petersburg gobelins from the series *Porte des Fleurs* as a gift from the Russian Empress Catharine II, which he integrated into the wall décor in 1778. The tapestries had to be folded back to fit them into the wall panels where they were set in carved gilded wall frames. With the exception of two large gobelins which have disappeared, they returned in 2002 as a loan.

To replace the **Staircase** with four flights (**Room 27**) from the time of Friedrich as Crown Prince, Carl Wilhelm Hennert, Director of Building Works, constructed the more representational staircase with two flights in the upper storey widened by a window

p. 24/25: Corps de Logis with pavilions

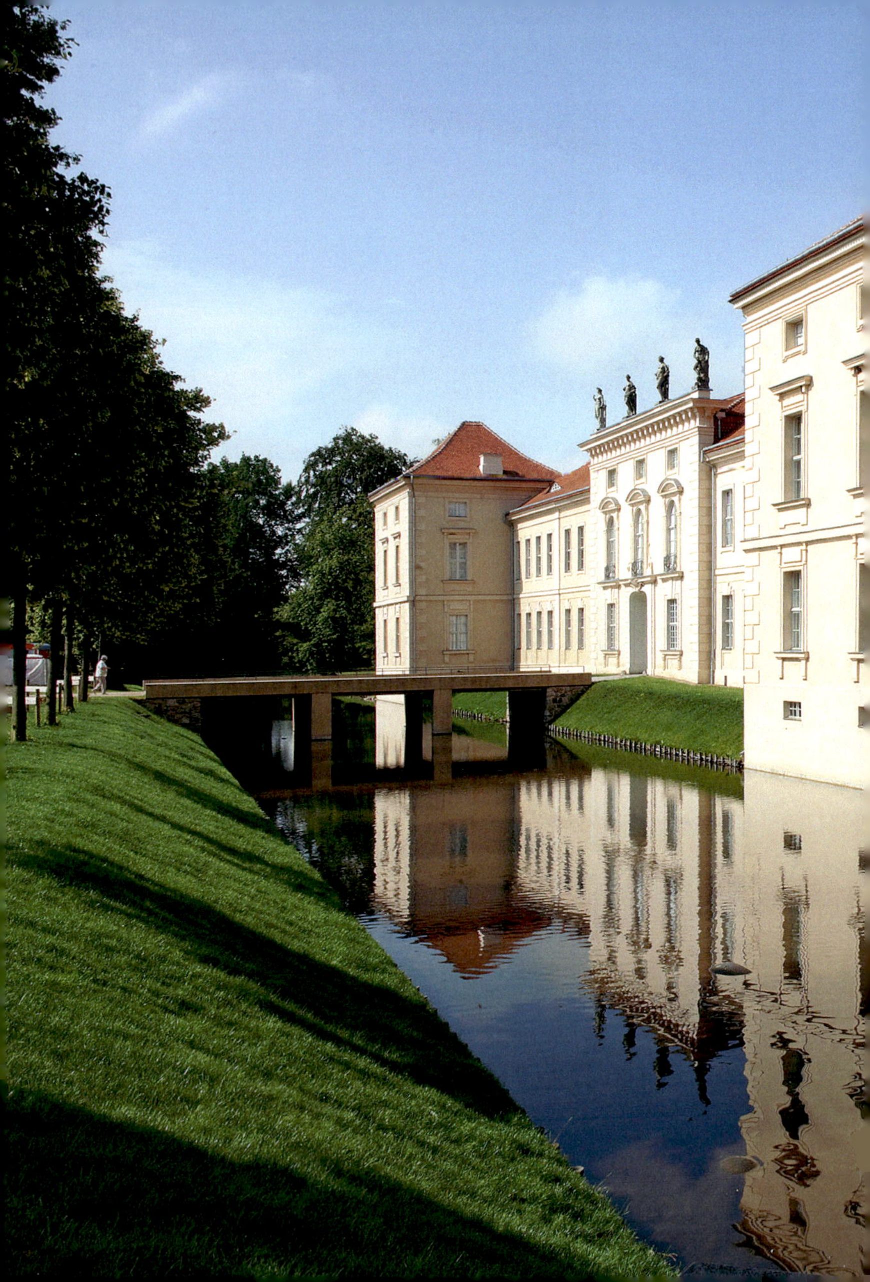

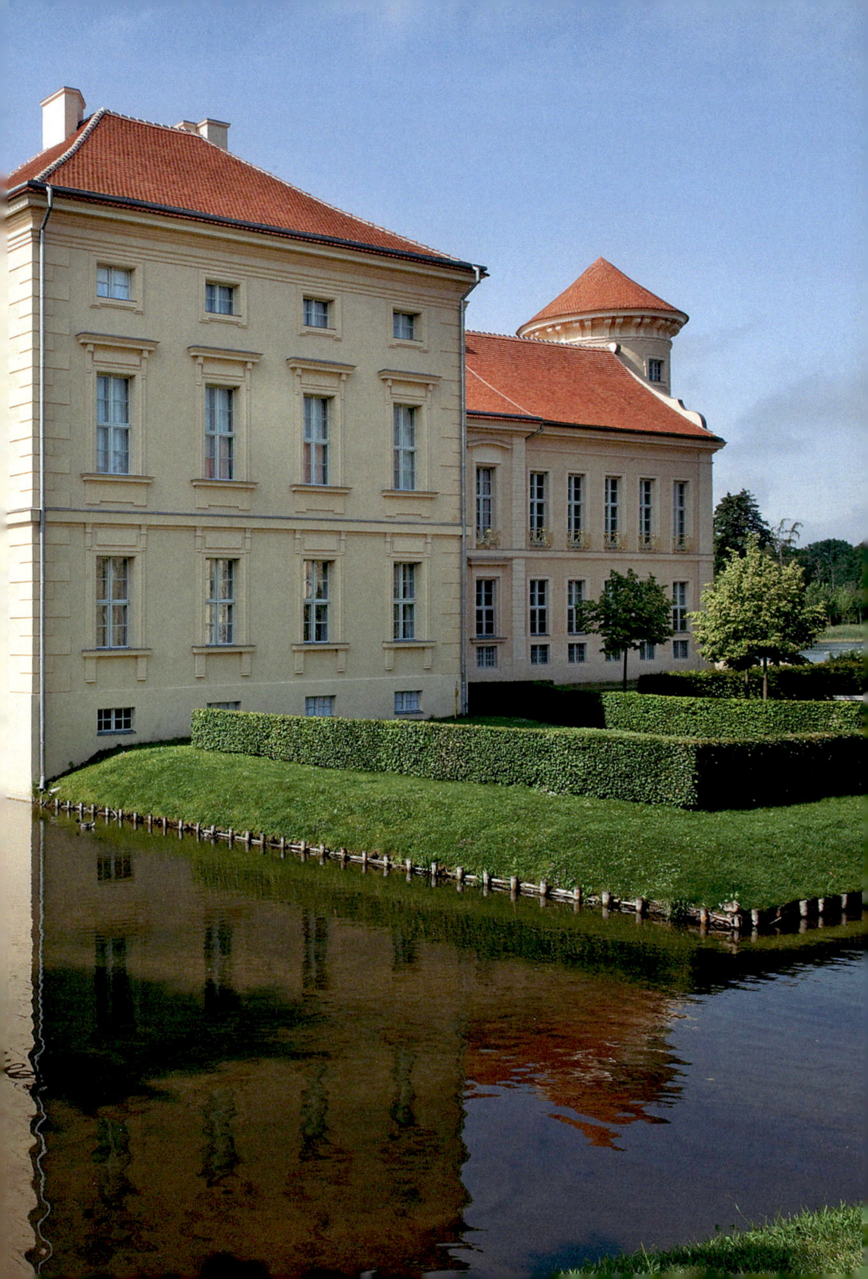

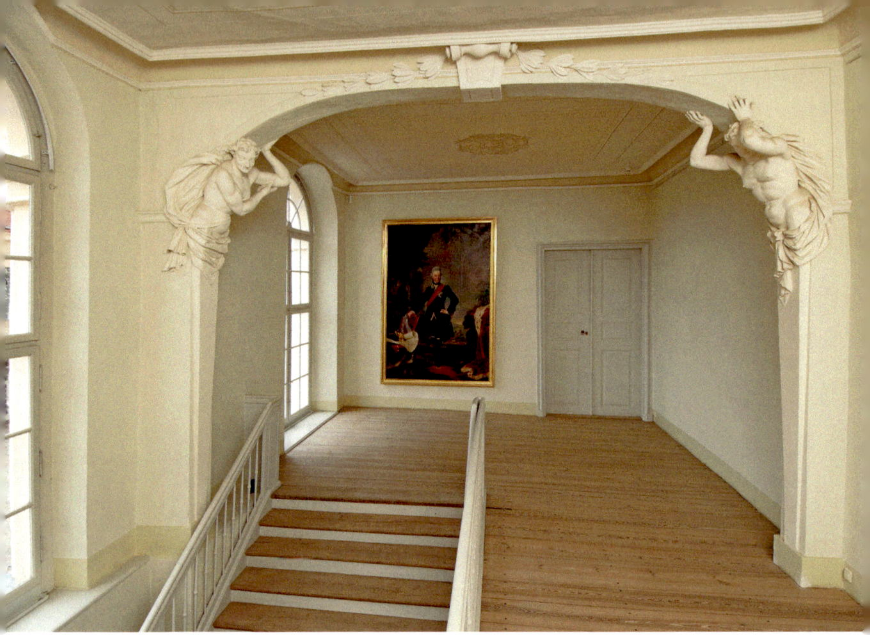

segment. The wall to the next room which was demolished was replaced by a transverse arch supported by figures of Atlas. Trompe-l'oeil Ionic pilasters, rectangular reserves and supraportes in the form of a laurel wreath underlined the neo-classical character of the new staircase. Above the staircase and hall there were two ceiling paintings with allegories of hunting and fishing by Friedrich Reclam, which were removed at the beginning of the 19th century in the course of remodelling. As the original banisters with latticework and garlands in chased bronze were replaced by the still extant wooden banisters, restoration was aimed at preserving the present visible decoration with its painted mouldings and central rosettes on the ceilings and the monochrome wall and door paints from the early 19th century. Only in the area of the ground floor and the landing have the exposed wall décors from the original building period been left visible.

Main staircase with a portrait of Prince Heinrich by Anna Dorothea Therbusch, c. 1723

## Apartment of Prince Heinrich (Rooms 28 to 43)

The **Anteroom or Rittersaal** (Knights' Hall) (**Room 28**) which has been preserved with its original décor (c. 1737/40) served as a vestibule to the apartment of the Crown Princess Elisabeth Christine. In the course of the restoration begun in 2004 the décor in pale blue and pink marbelised shades from the time of the Crown Prince on the wall coverings and doors was re-discovered. The ceiling painting *Mars und Venus* by Antoine Pesne determines the thematic design of the room. The medallions in relief above the doors show Hannibal, Caesar, Scipio and Pompey. The portraits of King Friedrich Wilhelm I and Queen Sophie Dorothea painted by Georg Wenzeslaus von Knobelsdorff (c. 1737) were part of the Crown Prince's furnishings of the room.

In 1769 the new **Marble or Shell Room** (**Room 29**) decorated with shell and coral festoons was created to replace the four living rooms of the Crown Princess under the direction of Carl Wilhelm Hennert, Director of Building Works, based on a design by Carl Gotthard Langhans, which has not been preserved. It is an unusually early example of the transition phase from rococo to early neo-classicism in Brandenburg.

The restored and in part reconstructed four console tables in front of the window pillars are a rare example of the originally sumptuous furnishings of the apartments. The glass candelabra (presumably Zechliner Hütte, after 1750) is a replacement for the chandeliers in the palace, all of which have disappeared.

The construction of the south east pavilion in 1785 gave Heinrich his third **library** room (**Room 30**). The collection of books previously housed in nine cupboards grew to more than 5000 volumes. The like-

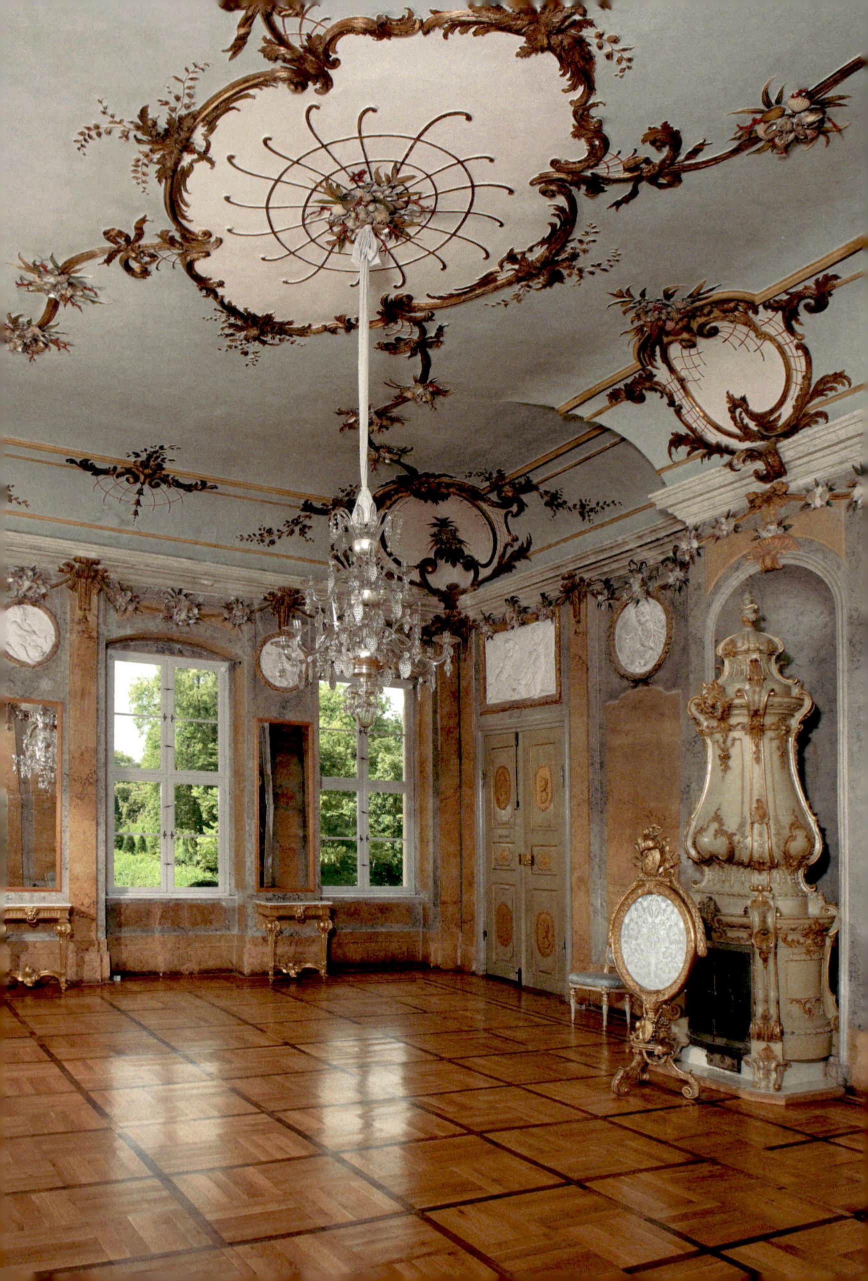

nesses of poets and scholars and ceiling portraits were also complemented by portrait busts by Jean Antoine Houdon. After the death of the Prince the books, works of art and furniture were sold to the Königliche Bibliothek zu Berlin (Royal Library). Since 2006 the still extant 14 portraits and three portrait busts have again been displayed here as a loan from the Staatsbibliothek Berlin.

The **Bedchamber** (**Room 31**) of Prince Heinrich was created around 1786 by amalgamating two smaller cabinets from the time of the Crown Prince. Heinrich's library was situated in the alcove area until the construction of the south east pavilion. The impression created by the room is determined by the striking textile wall-covering made of a woven silk fabric (Lampas) with a blue ground. Lace ribbons, vases of flowers and parrots are woven into the fabric in yellow and white. The neo-classical character is essentially determined by the frames on the two ceiling panels with coffering painted in perspective and grotesques painted on the panelling in the front half of the room. The execution of the décor, presumably by Bartholomeo Verona, was carried out using classical designs from Herculaneum and Pompeii from the collection in the Prince's library.

The **Lange Kammer** (Long Chamber) (**Room 32**) was created together with the other state rooms only in the course of extensive building works after 1786. The original »Golden Chamber« of the Crown Prince was extended by one window segment eastwards. Heinrich had the room decorated in the neo-classical style using the boiseries of the Friderician apartment, three existing supraportes and the gilded cherub reliefs created by Johann Carl Scheffler.

In place of the new bedchamber of the Crown Prince Heinrich had the **Schreibkabinett** (writing cabinet, **Room 33**) created after 1763 which is still preserved in its original décor. Six French gobelins

Shell room

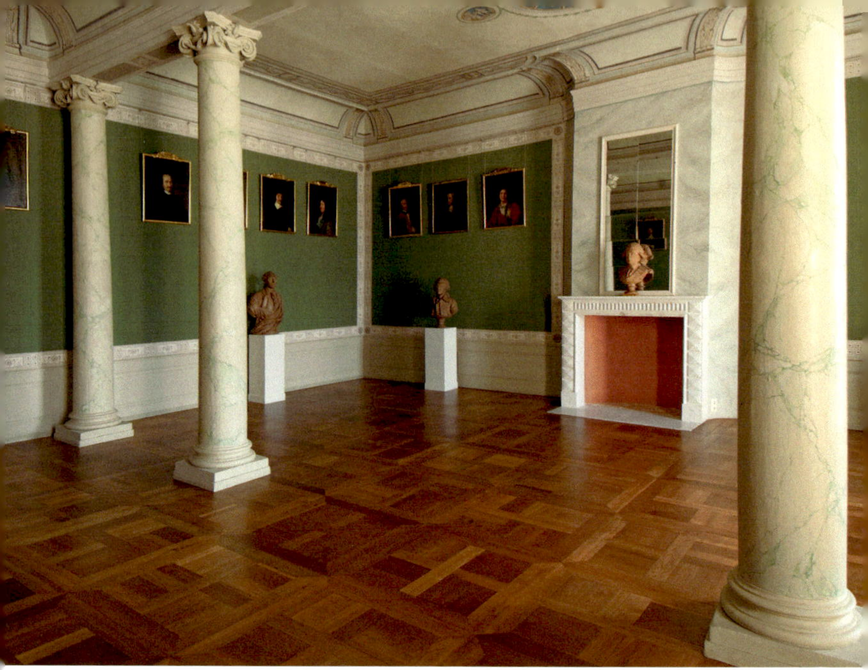

Prince Heinrich's Library

since lost from the Paris Savonnerie Manufactory, which Heinrich received as a gift in 1784 from Ludwig XVI during his first visit to France, adorned the wall panels. The present furnishings of the room again include the portrait of Queen Sophie Dorothea, which Antoine Pesne presented to the Crown Prince in Rheinsberg on 8 November, 1737. The painting with the view of Rheinsberg by Georg Wenzeslaus von Knobelsdorff (c. 1735) shows the palace before it was converted into the official residence of the Crown Prince.

The **Picture Gallery** (**Room 24**) created after 1763 involved abandoning the first Banqueting Room from the time of the Crown Prince. Only the mantlepiece designed by Georg Wenzeslaus von Knobelsdorff was retained from the former Hall of Mirrors of the Crown Prince's apartment. The wall panelling and parts of

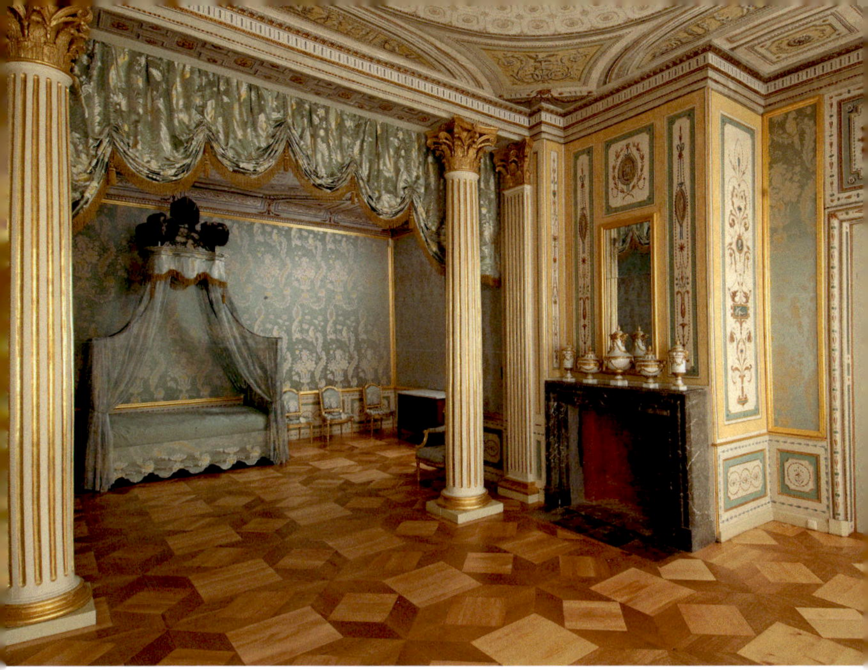

State bedchamber of Prince Heinrich

the marquetry flooring from this reconstruction have survived. Of the ceiling décor only the preliminary drawings by the stucco master and several stucco fragments have been preserved. In 1802 there were 50 paintings in this room alone by Antoine Pesne, Nicolas Lancret and Jean-Baptiste-Marie Pierre among others. Acquisitions and loans have brought back eight paintings from the Prince's collection to the gallery.

The windowless **Entree** (**Room 36**) came into being as a result of the creation of the picture gallery. During the restoration works in the early 1990s fragments of the original room design from the time of the Crown Prince were detected. Friedrich had a large room created in front of his tower cabinet spanning the entire width of the Klingenberg wing. The design of the doors with their silver-painted rhombus pat-

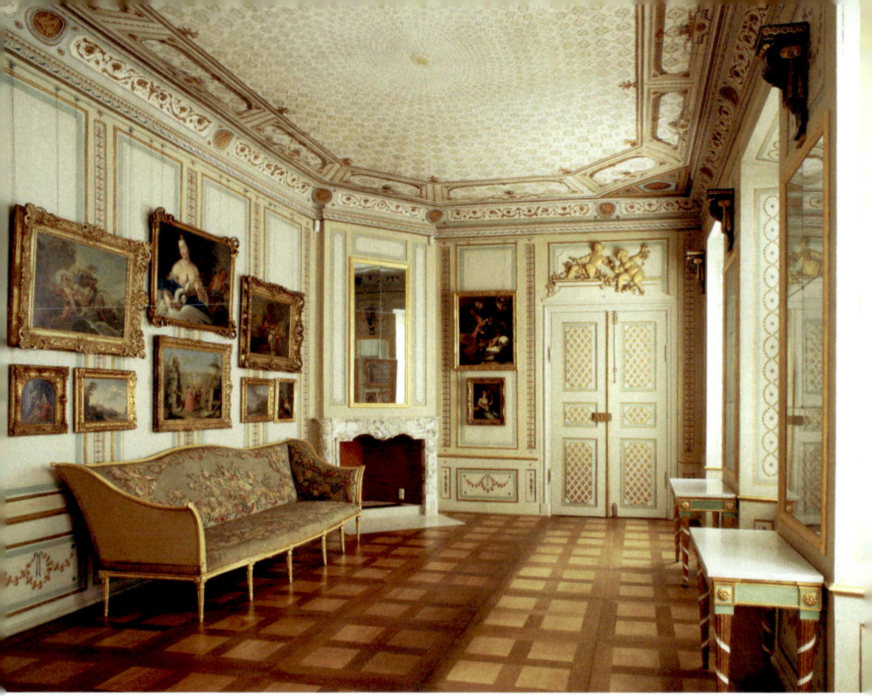

tern and the wall decoration with its silver-grey grisaille painting give an impression of what the earlier room design was like.

Long chamber

The **Tower Cabinet** (**Room 35**) on the top floor of the old, already existing Klingenberg tower was used as a library by Friedrich. The ceiling painting by Antoine Pesne *Minerva als Beschützerin von Wissenschaft und Kunst* (*Minerva as Protectress of Science and Art)* and the gilded carvings by Johann Carl Scheffler – attributes of the arts and science – have been preserved from the time of the Crown Prince. The Crown Prince's collection of books, which was probably kept in book shelves in front of the walls, was taken to Potsdam in 1747 where Friedrich II had a library created in a round room at Schloss Sanssouci, which was modelled on the Rheinsberg library. The

Tower cabinet, Crown Prince's Library

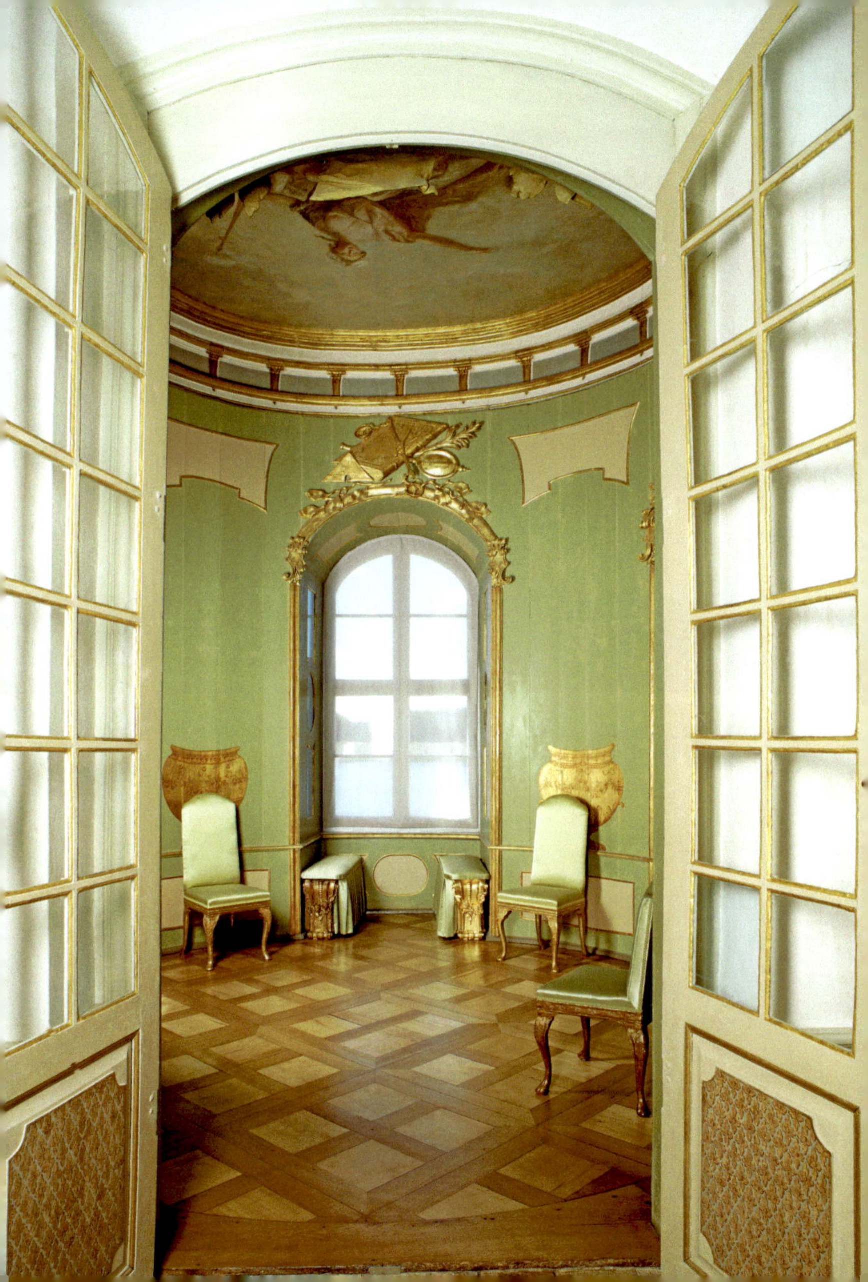

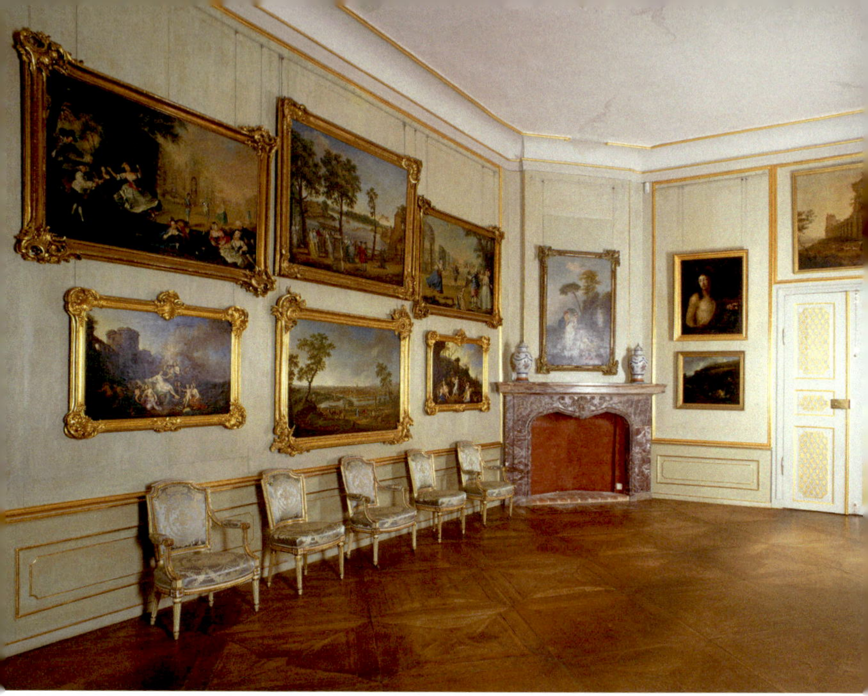

design, today represented by a replica, was commissioned in 1769 by Prince Heinrich. The window seats (c. 1766, replica of 2002) were presumably part of this design.

Picture gallery

## GROUND FLOOR

The palace room designated as **Billiard Room** (**Room 50**) in the inventory of 1742 with its vaulted ceiling is a vestige of the earlier building. The two glazed outer doors make it an optical link between the palace and the garden. Looking south the observer sees the unique garden layout created by von Knobelsdorff, which extends over the Billiard bridge into the main baroque avenue to the ornamental garden gate, whereby the motif of the putti on the groups of columns echo the figures of putti on the mantlepiece in the room.

Prince Heinrich had the two **Vaulted Chambers** (**Rooms 48 and 49**) painted in the trompe l'oeil fashion in 1771 by Friedrich Reclam who presumably brought most of the motifs used here as sketches from his several years' study in Rome.

The chamber next to the Billard Room simulates a rocky grotto with views of the landscape panorama of Tivoli with the Temple of the Vestal Virgins and the Grande Cascata (great cascade).

In the second chamber, an evocation of a vaulted room from Antiquity, there are also trompe l'oeil sculptures and reliefs of famous classical works of art painted on the walls, for example the Venus Kallipygos on the left next to the door. During the time the palace was used as a sanatorium, in which these rooms were used as wet rooms for physiotherapeutic treatments, they were painted over several times and in the grotto room large sections of wall décor were completely lost. The restoration of the remains that were preserved was completed in 2004.

## Summer Apartment of Prince Heinrich (**Rooms 51 to 62**)

The ground floor rooms originally included apartments for members of the Crown Prince's circle of friends. Heinrich too used them as »chambers for guests« until from 1785 he finally had his private apartments installed here.

Three rooms with chinoiserie décor were part of the summer apartment. Unfortunately, in the **Chinese Chamber** (**Room 51**) only the original Chinese paper wall hanging from the 18th century was preserved. It shows various exotic flowering trees with

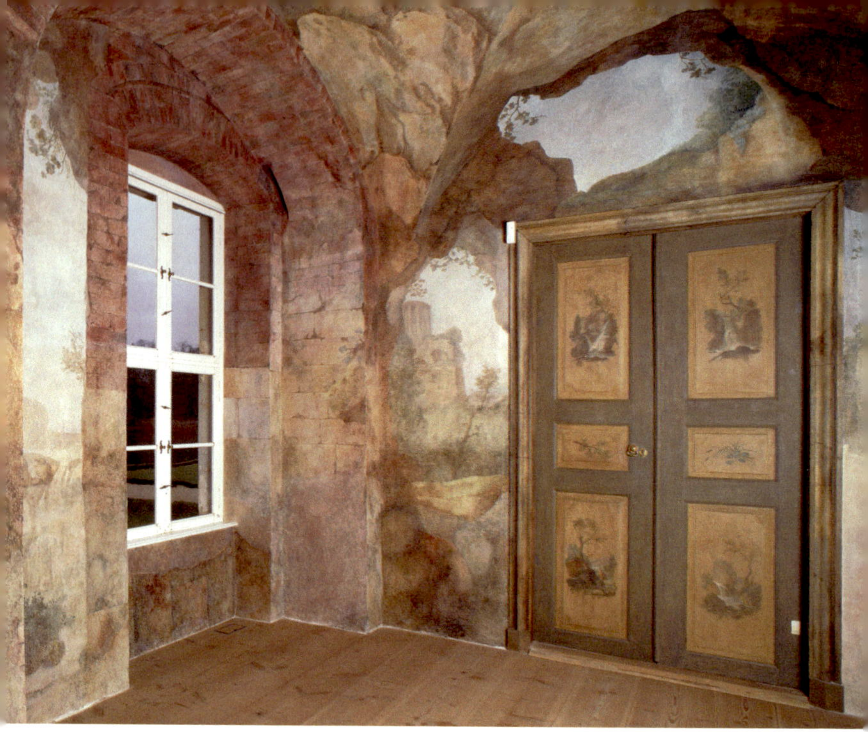

birds and insects. Even though the splendid colour of the wallpaper was lost in the course of time, the visitor can after painstaking restoration again sense the overall impression made by the room in the late 18th century.

Vaulted chamber, grotto room

The **White Painted Chamber** (**Room 52**) decorated in the neo-classical style was created in 1785 in the context of the pavilion-like extensions. The wall-panelling which is still in its original place has a chinoiserie design on the reverse side. The painting was no longer felt to be fashionable and was sacrificed to the sober monochrome décor by turning and converting the boiserie in 1785. The stucco reliefs with scenes from classical mythology and history, the two portrait busts by Jean Antoine Houdon of Louis Jules Mancini,

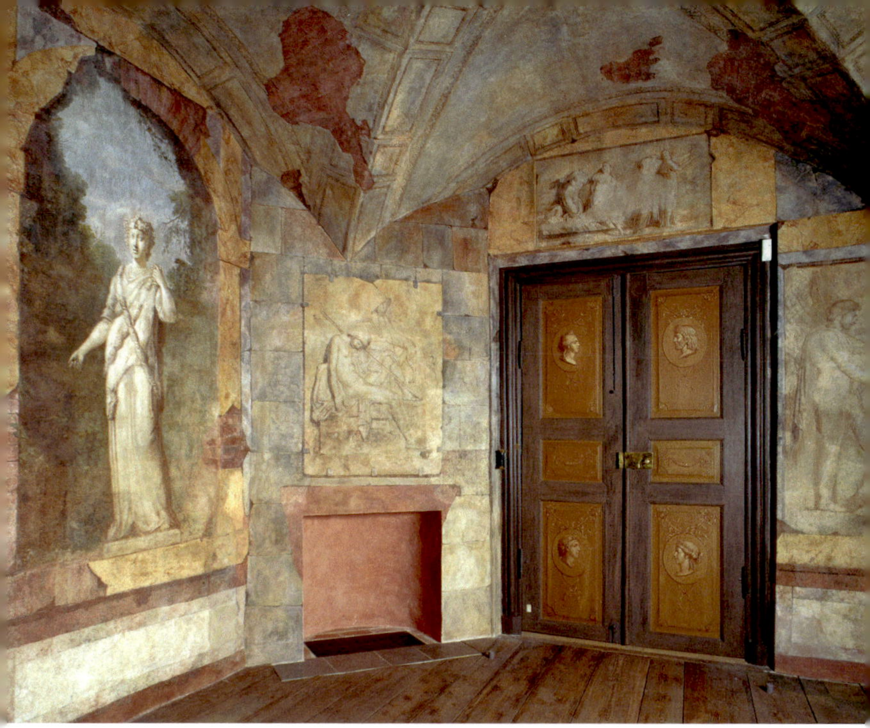

Vaulted chamber, classical room

Duc de Nivernais (c. 1787) and Françoise Eléonore Comtesse de Sabran (c. 1785), who is also shown in a painting again hung here by Elisabeth Vigée-Lebrun (1786), and the bust of Queen Ulrike Luise of Sweden (1781/1782) by Johann Tobias Sergel are part of the original furnishings of the room.

In the pavilion that was built on in 1785 a **Gallery Room** (**Room 53**) was created, which with white painted boiseries likewise had a sober neo-classical décor. With the exception of parts of the ceiling the furnishings were destroyed by building works after 1950. A museum-style presentation shows the lost furnishings of the Berlin Palace of Prince Heinrich.

Prince Heinrich had a Chinese medallion wallpaper, which was made in the fashion of »print-room«

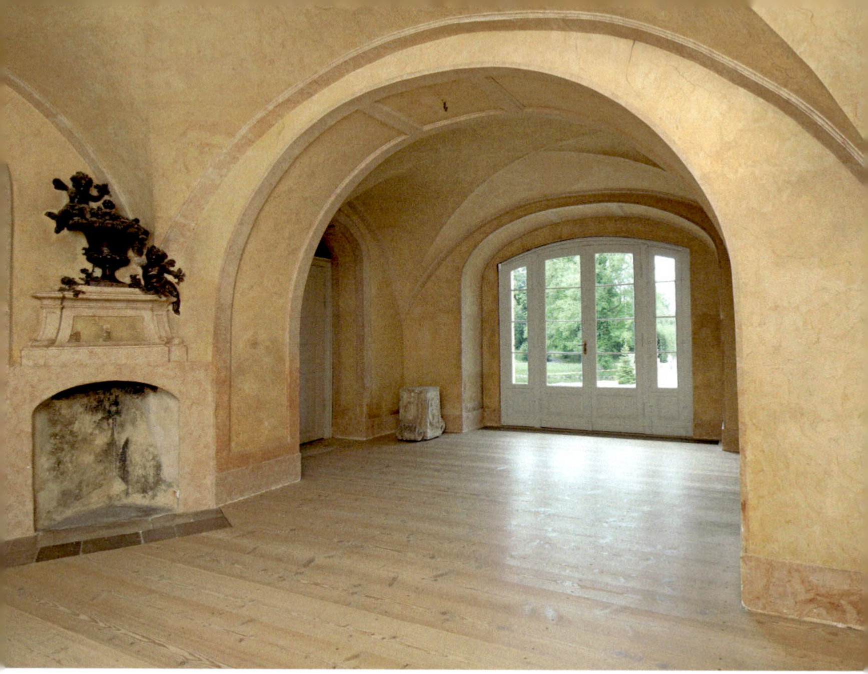

Billiard room

papers and was imported around 1788, hung in his new **Writing Chamber** (**Room 54**), to which four pieces of furniture for writing belonged. The ceiling painting with its impressive colour transitions, which was the only original décor element to be partly preserved under the later coats of paint, contained references to the floral frames of the wallpaper, which was removed from the room after 1945. In the restoration of the room it was only possible to reconstruct the original basic colour of the paper.

Behind the **Cabinet** (**Room 55**) there was a small linking staircase which gave direct access from the library located in the upper storey to the summer apartment. This connection between the book collection and the small cabinet situated below it as a link between the representational rooms in the upper story and the private apartments of the Prince ex-

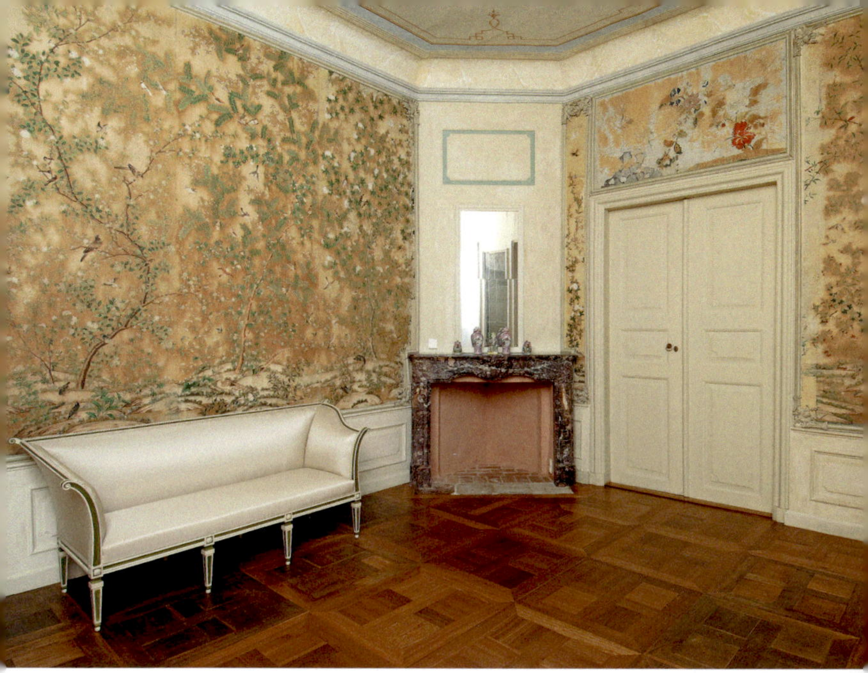

Summer apartment, Chinese chamber

plains the selection of 101 pictures which used to be hung here, which are tantamount to a Memorial Temple of Friendship. 31 portraits with theatrical subjects were the expression of the Prince's love of the theatre. Beneath them hung the painting by Nicolas Lancret with the title *Die Tänzerin Maria Sallé* (the dancer Maria Sallé) (1732), which it was possible to buy back in 2001 with the support of the Kulturstiftung der Länder, the Ernst von Siemens Kunst-Fonds and the Friends of the Preußische Schlösser und Gärten e.V.

Presumably in the course of the redesigning of the adjacent rooms the Prince also had his **Bedchamber** (**Room 57**) modernised around 1786, whereby he took over the mantlepiece which was made in in 1737 after a design by Georg Wenzeslaus von Knobelsdorff. Ionic pilasters and two wooden Ionic columns sepa-

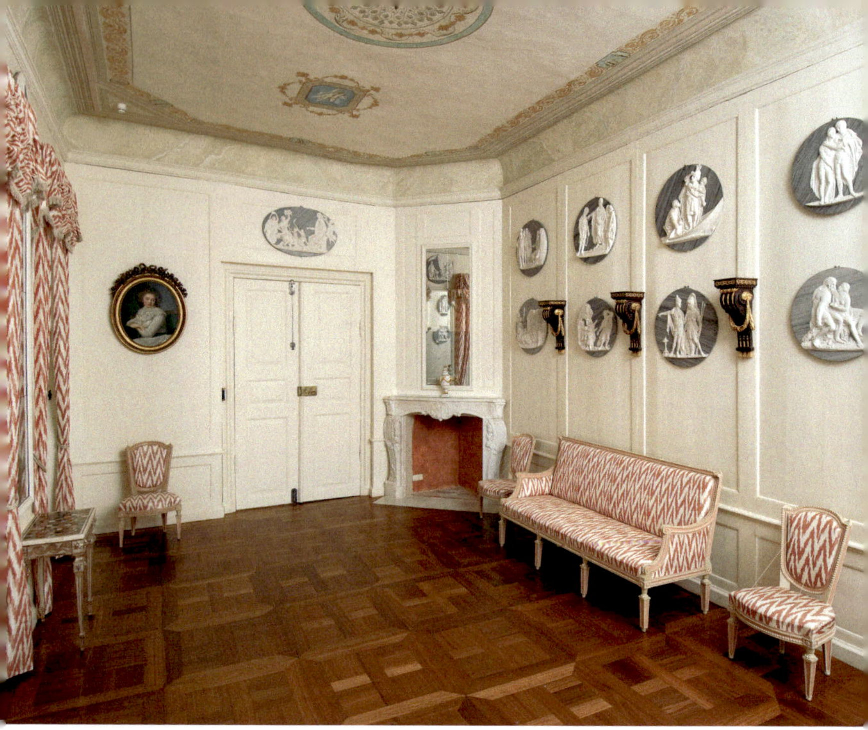

rate the alcove from the rest of the room. The ceiling painting clearly alludes to the function of the room (owls and bats as creatures of the night in the central ornament, goddesses with attributes such as a snake or poppy capsules as guardians of health and sleep in the corner medallions). Apart from a rich selection of furniture the inventory of 1802 also lists 42 paintings of which a large part was sold by auction in the 19th century. The two supraportes by an unknown painter replace two still lifes by Augustin Dubuisson, which disappeared as late as 1945. Prince Heinrich died on 3 August 1802 in this room.

Summer apartment, white painted room

Heinrich had the **Chinese Cabinet** (**Room 60**) furnished as early as around 1760. Presumably the Chinese wallpaper with flower and bird motifs and the

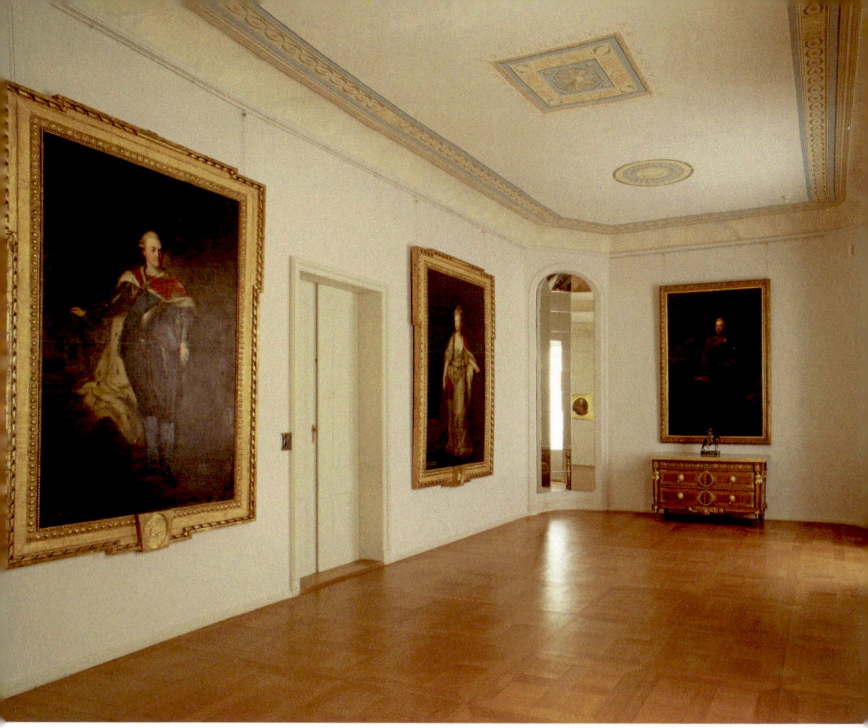

Summer apartment, gallery

wallpaper for the Chinese Chamber were imported to Germany as early as 1754. As a result of the extensive and invasive reconstruction work in connection with the installation of the sanatorium in the 1950s the original design of the room was destroyed with the exception of a few details such as the cornice. The sandstone chimneypiece, the Chinese wallpaper and the panelling decorated with chinoiseries were removed. After 1945 it was possible to take the chimneypiece showing a Chinese couple and part of the frame for safe-keeping to Potsdam Sanssouci. The two painted door leaves were discovered at the beginning of the 90s in the coach house in the courtyard of the Kavaliershaus – being used as a coal shed (restoration completed 2002).

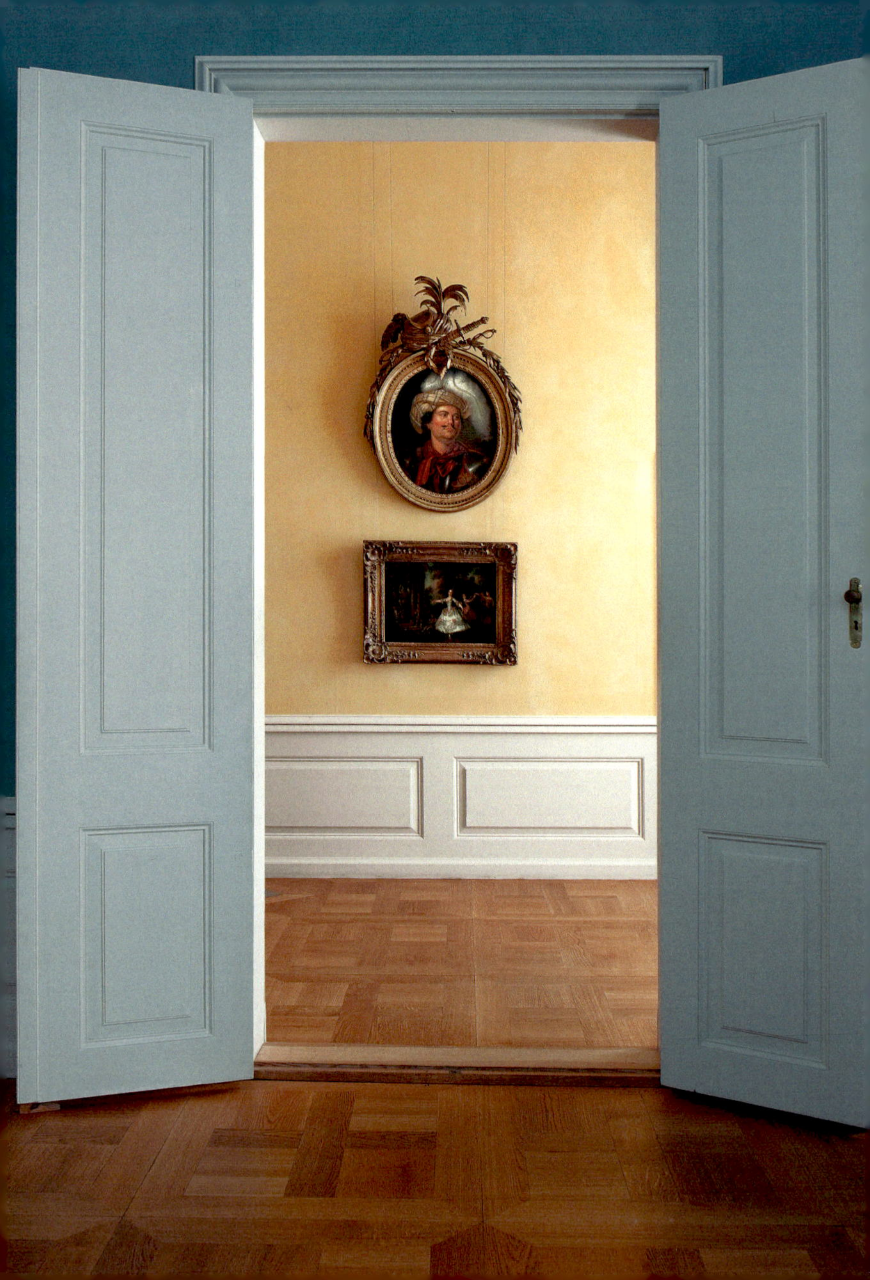

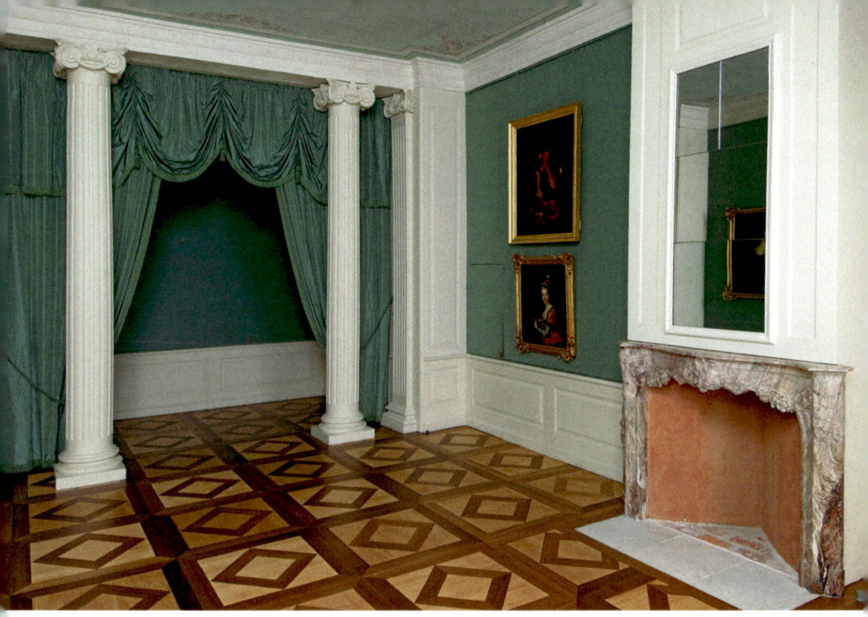

Summer apartment, bedchamber

Small cabinet with Nicolas Lancret: The dancer Maria Sallé, 1732

The visitor has access to the Palace entrance via the **cloakroom** (**Room 62**), which in the inventory of 1802 is described as being hung »mit alt grün Papier«. A photo documentation from 1990 shows the Palace rooms during their use as a sanatorium.

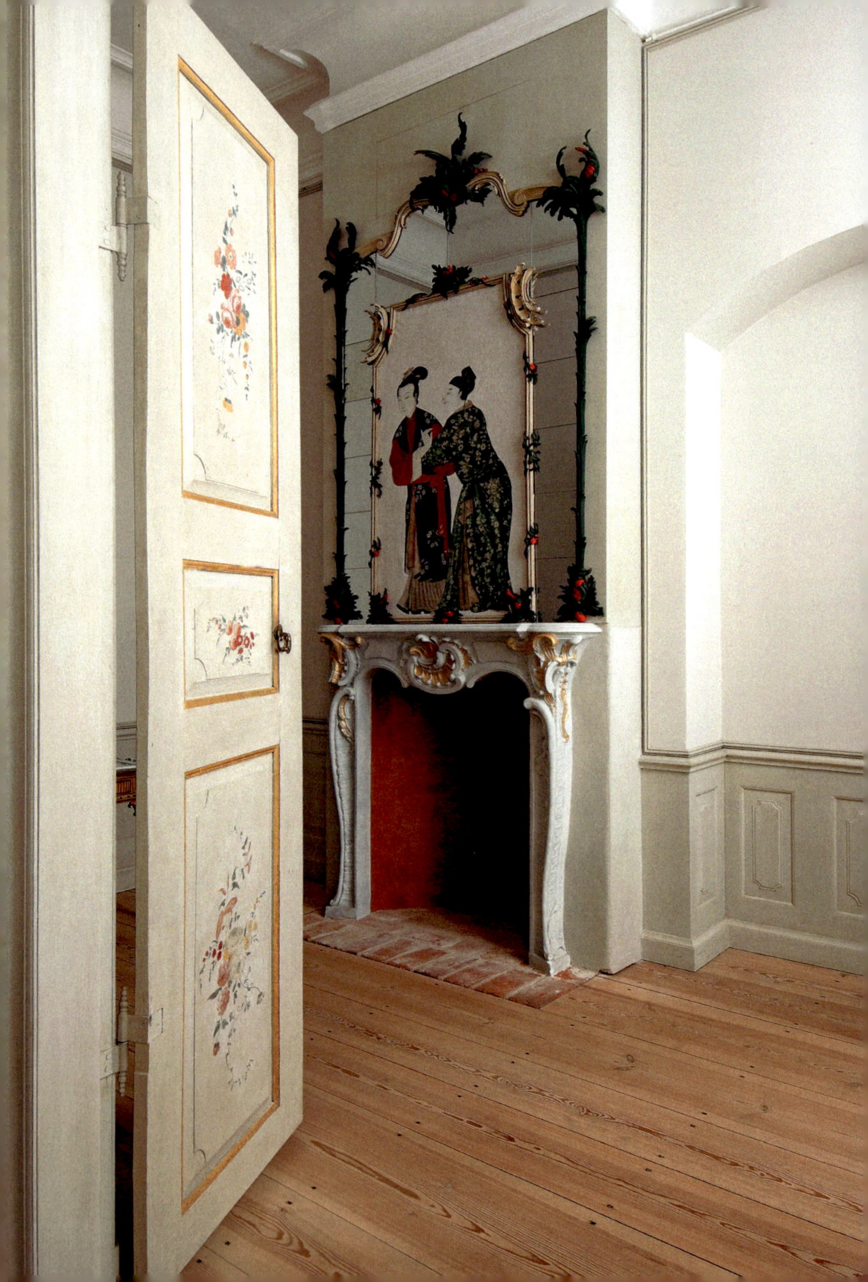

**Schloss Rheinsberg**
Mühlenstraße 1
D-16831 Rheinsberg

## Contact details

Stiftung Preußische Schlösser und Gärten
Berlin Brandenburg
Visitor Service Schloss Rheinsberg
Information
Mühlenstraße 1
1683 Rheinsberg
Tel: + 49 (0) 33931.7260
Fax: +49 (0) 33931.72626

## Group reservations

Tel.: +49 (0) 33931. 7269
Fax: +49 (0) 33931.72626
Email: h.heldt@spsg.de

## Opening times and admission charges

Schloss Rheinsberg is open from Tuesday to Sunday. Current opening times and admission charges on www.spsg.de.

The visitor information service at Schloss Rheinsberg will be pleased to provide updates on admission charges for groups, range of guided tours and special events.

The Kurt Tucholsky Literaturmuseum is likewise located at Schloss Rheinsberg. Admission is included in the admission charge for Schloss Rheinsberg. The »Kavalierhaus« (apartments for the courtly household) and the Marstall (stables) are also part of the

Summer apartment, Chinese cabinet

palace ensemble. The Reception Area with the service counter and museum shop are located in the Marstall, which was originally built to accomodate horses and carriages.

The »Kavalierhaus« is used by the Musikakademie Rheinsberg GmbH. The Akademie regularly organises concerts, opera and ballet performances and a wide variety of other events in the Schlosstheater Rheinsberg, the palace's historic Hall of Mirrors, the park and in the courtyard of the academy.

Every year from the end of June to the middle of August the Kammeroper (chamber opera) Schloss Rheinsberg organises the International Festival of Young Opera Singers with unforgettable opera evenings, some of them in the Heckentheater (theatre in the hedge enclosures) in the gardens or in the courtyard of the palace.

## How to get there

From Berlin: by RE train from Berlin Hauptbahnhof (main station) direct link from April to October to Rheinsberg Station, or Neuruppin and continuing journey by bus. Information on www.Reiseauskunft.bahn.de

By car via A24 (Autobahn) to exit Neuruppin, then via B167 and B122 to Rheinsberg.

## Information for visitors with impaired mobility

Access to Schloss Rheinsberg and Kurt Tucholsky Literary Museum for visitors with impaired mobility ♿.

Access to the Schlosstheater im Kavalierhaus ♿.

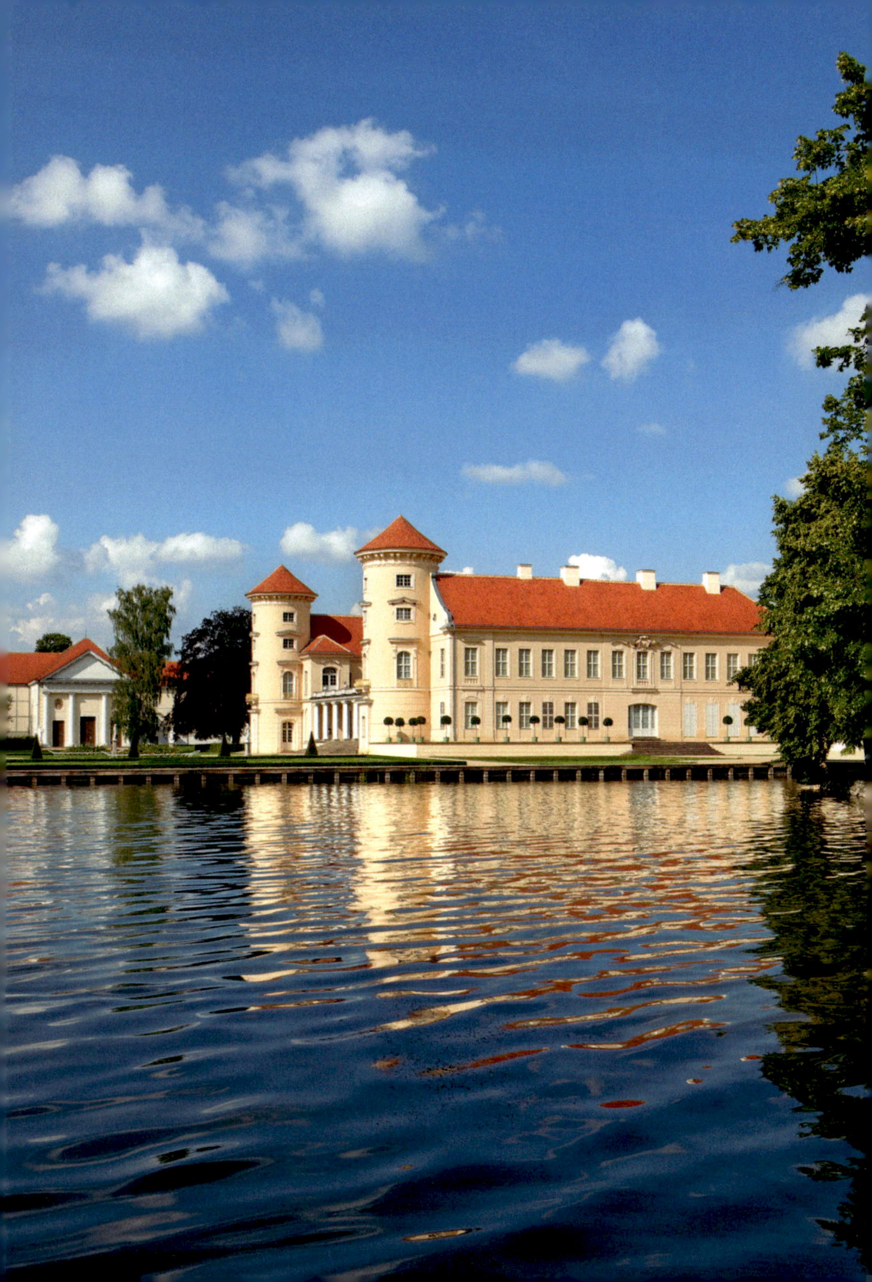

Acknowledgments

Published by the Stiftung Preußische Schlösser und Gärten Berlin-Brandenburg
Text: Claudia Sommer, Detlef Fuchs (Palace)
Michael Rhode (Garden)
Editor: Martin Steinbrück
Translation: Ulrich Boltz/Richard Gary Hooton
Design: M&S Hawemann
Set by: Hendrik Bäßler
Production: Jens Möbius
Coordination: Elvira Kühn
Fotos: Bildarchiv SPSG/fotografer: Daniel Lindner, Roland Handrick, Wolfgang Pfauder, Leo Seidel

Die Deutsche Nationalbibliothek verzeichnet diese Publikation in der Deutschen Nationalbibliografie; detaillierte bibliografische Daten sind im Internet über http://dnb.d-nb.de abrufbar.


ISBN 978-3-422-04008-3